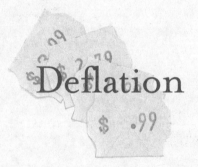

Deflation

Collins

An Imprint of HarperCollins*Publishers*

Deflation

WHAT HAPPENS
WHEN PRICES
FALL

Chris Farrell

HarperCollins books may be purchased for educational, business,
or sales promotional use. For information, please write to:
Special Markets Department, HarperCollins Publishers,
10 East 53rd Street, New York, New York 10022.

First Collins paperback edition 2005.

Designed by William Ruoto

The Library of Congress has catalogued the
hardcover edition as follows:

Library of Congress Cataloging-in-Publication Data
Farrell, Chris.
Deflation : what happens when prices fall / Chris Farrell.
p.   cm.
Includes index.
ISBN 0-06-057645-6 (alk. paper)
1. Deflation (Finance).   I. Title.
HG229.F324   2004
332.4'1—dc22   2004040528

ISBN-10: 0-06-057646-4 (paperback)
ISBN-13: 978-0-06-057646-2

05 06 07 08 09   DIX/RRD   10 9 8 7 6 5 4 3 2 1

For
Peter and Connor

Acknowledgments

William Wolman, my longtime managing editor at *Business Week*, was fond of quoting famed sportswriter Red Smith whenever a deadline loomed on a big story: "Remember what Red Smith said, 'All you have to do is sit down at a typewriter and open a vein.'" I recalled Bill's admonition several times these past few months.

Yet writing a book is also a wonderfully collaborative undertaking. I got a great deal of support and encouragement from many people. At the top of the list is veteran prize-winning freelance financial reporter Ann Therese Palmer. A. T. did all the reporting on the automobile supply industry that makes up much of chapter 9. She also sent me a steady stream of reports, articles, insights, and humor over the past several months.

Several people read parts of the draft. Thanks to Arthur Rolnick, senior vice president and head of research at the Federal Reserve Bank of Minneapolis; Stephen Smith, managing editor at American RadioWorks, the public radio documentary production unit; Margaret Brower, director of productions at Public Radio International; and Ronald Jepperson, professor of sociology at Tulsa University.

Sound Money is a one-hour personal finance show produced by Minnesota Public Radio (MPR) and syndicated nationwide. The *Sound Money* crew at MPR—Kathryn Scott, Stephanie Curtis, Kara McGuire, and Nicholas Kereakos—were extremely thoughtful and helpful. So were Bill Buzenberg, senior vice president, news; Jon McTaggart, chief operating officer; and William Kling, president (all at MPR). At *Business Week,* Doug Harbrecht, executive editor, *Business Week* Online, and Beth Belton, news editor, *Business Week* Online, seemed to always understand whenever I had to call and take a pass on my weekly column. Michael Mandel, chief economist at *Business Week* magazine, was a constant resource of critical insight—and good cheer.

They don't know it, but the book club I belong to is a source of inspiration, partly for their love of reading books and partly for their love of conversation about books. I also understand that even though I've missed several months of meetings, I haven't been kicked out. Thanks to Alan Wilensky, Carolyn Levitt, David Buran, Jack Forsythe, Gailen Krug, Malcolm McDonald, Maria Jette, Michael O'Keefe, Philip Brunelle, Pat Harvey, Sandra Gardebring, Siobhan Cleary, and William Hogan.

Joelle Delbourgo is a terrific agent. Editor Marion Maneker not only hired me but stayed remarkably calm and reassuring throughout the process.

This book is dedicated to the two best young men I know and love, Peter and Connor.

Contents

Deflation

CHAPTER 1

"An Unwelcome Substantial Fall in Inflation"

> All is flux, nothing stays still. Nothing
> endures but change.
>
> —HERACLITUS

 MAY 6, 2003, WAS AN EXTRAORDINARY DAY IN Washington, D.C. The Federal Reserve held its Federal Open Market Committee (FOMC) meeting in its two-storied chandeliered boardroom at the central bank's white marble temple on Constitution Avenue. Now, there was nothing unusual about the FOMC gathering. The committee meets eight times a year to take the pulse of the economy and decide on monetary policy. The central bankers had a lot to talk about that day. The economy was struggling to gain traction following the implosion of the high-tech sector in the spring of 2000, the terrorist attack of 9/11, the recession, the recovery that felt like a recession, and the geoeconomic turmoil surrounding the U.S.-led invasions of Afghanistan and Iraq.

Still, the Fed had aggressively cut its benchmark interest rate 12 times since early 2001 to 1.25%—its lowest level since 1961. Most Wall Street soothsayers predicted the Fed members would vote to stay the course. Conventional wisdom was right. The FOMC kept monetary policy unchanged.

What made the day memorable in U.S. economic history was a phrase in the FOMC statement released right after the meeting: "The probability of an unwelcome substantial fall in inflation, though minor, exceeds that of a pickup in inflation from its already low level." Okay, "an unwelcome substantial fall in inflation" is hardly the sort of incendiary declaration that typically heralds revolutionary change. It lacks the punch of Karl Marx's "Workers of the world unite!" or Franklin Roosevelt's "There is nothing to fear but fear itself."

Yet the arid phrase "an unwelcome substantial fall in inflation"—a new euphemism for falling prices—stunned financiers, executives, and policy-makers around the world. It signaled a tectonic shift in the American economy. The most powerful economic institution in the world, led by Alan Greenspan, a legendary practitioner of the central banking craft, was no longer worried about accelerating inflation, capitalism's main economic villain of the past six decades. No, for the first time since the Great Depression of the 1930s, the specter haunting the Fed was deflation, a widespread, persistent decline in the average price level.

A few weeks later Greenspan abandoned any linguistic pretense. "We at the Federal Reserve recognize that deflation is a possibility," Greenspan testified before Congress. "Even though we perceive the risks as minor, the potential consequences are very substantial and could be quite negative."[1]

Deflation is an unfamiliar, unsettling bogeyman—with good reason. America's most notorious episode of deflation was also its last—the Great Depression. There was a brief but largely forgotten episode in 1954–55. For most people, deflation is synonymous with a depression, an economic collapse, a social catastrophe. The terms *deflation* and *depression* are almost interchangeable. The prospect of a widespread decline in prices evoked disturbing images from the 1930s of soup kitchens for the unemployed and dispossessed, a stock market crash, and shuttered banks.

Of course, fringe forecasters like economist Ravi Batra, journalist Sir William Rees-Mogg, and market timer Robert Prechter had long warned about coming deflations, depressions, and economic Armageddons. Doomsaying made for the best-seller list, but most people rightly ignored these perpetual Chicken Littles. After all, one of Batra's best-selling books predicted a great depression starting in 1990. Oops. There had been brief scares that stirred unsettling parallels to the catastrophe in the 1930s, such as the stock market crash of October 19, 1987, and the savings and loan crisis of the late 1980s. But since both financial shocks failed to presage a major collapse in economic activity, most policy makers and economists quickly dismissed the odds of deflation or depression. The rare exceptions included the extremely astute economist and commentator Paul Krugman in *The Return of Depression Economics* and investment strategist A. Gary Shilling in *Deflation.*[2]

Yet all of a sudden in the spring of 2003 it wasn't hard for mainstream Wall Street economists to sketch a picture of an America—or the global economy for that matter—on the precipice of a destructive deflationary spiral. "Like it or not, we are in uncharted waters, both in diagnosing the world's problems as well as in prescribing the remedies," said Stephen Roach, chief economist at the blue chip investment bank Morgan Stanley. "I never dreamt that I would live to see such profound challenges."[3] Added David Rosenberg, chief North American economist for Merrill Lynch: "The concern for central bankers is whether a deflationary psychology takes hold that causes expectations of lower prices to fuel lower prices down the road and hence trigger a 'deflationary spiral.'"[4]

What changed? Arithmetic, for one thing. Inflation, or a sustained rise in the overall price level, had been running between 1% and 2%, and 1% is close to zero and zero is close to negative prices or deflation. For another, the economy exhibited some disturbingly eerie parallels to the experience of the 1920s expansion and the 1930s depression.

The 1920s were an optimistic, adventurous decade. A "new economy" emerged, largely fueled by the automobile, electric power, and appliances such as refrigerators and radios. Inflation was dormant and trade between nations flourished. Big business invested enormous sums in plants and equipment to take advantage of the efficiency promise of mass production techniques and mass marketing tactics. Worker productivity soared by some 40%, and real (inflation-adjusted) earnings gained 23%. Prosperity allowed the government to plow budget surpluses into paying off the national debt and reduce the top income tax rate from 65% to 32%, as well as slash capital gains taxes. Investment in education doubled during the decade, much of it concentrated on secondary education. The percent of 17-year-olds with a high school diploma jumped from 16% to 26%. And the number of male college graduates more than doubled, while the ranks of their female peers with a sheepskin almost tripled.[5]

The long expansion raised living standards and transformed the quality of everyday life. Automobile registrations went from around 9 million in 1921 to more than 23 million in 1929. The number of radios in homes soared from a handful to 10 million over the same time period.[6] The average home now had running water, electric lights, and a bathtub. Thanks to the growing acceptance of consumer credit—buy now, pay later—many families no longer had to wait years to purchase the latest household gadgets, such as washing machines and dishwashers. "The transition from a 'home-made' to a 'store-bought' world of goods was an economic revolution that profoundly affected values of all kinds," writes historian Maury Klein in *Rainbow's End*. "Among other changes it ushered in an age of materialism with a vastly broader base of participants than had ever existed in America or anywhere else."[7]

Investors embraced the new economy with enthusiasm. Stock market prices spiraled higher, and the middle class bought equities in a big way for the first time. Wall Street promoters encouraged customers to buy equities on "margin," or with borrowed money. The pitch was that stocks only went up. The *Saturday Evening Post* satirically captured the legendary speculative binge in the spring and summer of 1929.[8]

Oh, hush thee, my babe, granny's bought some more shares
Daddy's gone to play with the bulls and the bears,
Mother's buying on tips, and she simply can't lose.
And baby shall have some expensive new shoes.

It has a familiar ring, doesn't it? Then, as we all know, the stock market collapsed in 1929, followed by the Great Depression and the deflation of the 1930s.

Now, let's fast forward to the new economy of the 1990s. Innovation flourished, with the longest economic expansion in U.S. history driven by business investment in software, computer networks, the Internet, and other advanced information technologies. The economy grew at a 3.3% annual rate during the expansion that ended in 2001. Wages for private-sector workers adjusted for inflation gained 1.3% a year. Productivity growth accelerated to an average yearly pace of 2.2%, about double the performance of the previous two decades. The percent of adults 25 years or older with four or more years of college rose from 21% in 1991 to 26% in 2001.[9] The unemployment rate plunged, and the number of Americans living in poverty dropped dramatically. The federal government's budget deficit turned into a surplus, and the inflation rate dropped from 4.2% in 1991 to 2.8% in 2001.

The vast majority of Americans never had it so good. Home ownership soared to record heights, with almost 68% of households owning their home compared to 64% in 1991. A third of families owned three or more cars. Chains like Target, Crate and Barrel, Restoration Hardware, and Bed, Bath, and Beyond offered good design at reasonable prices. Cell phones let parents go out and leave their children with a babysitter without constantly worrying if everything was okay. The Internet allowed Americans to research all kinds of products free of any hard sales tactics. Consumer credit was plentiful.

The stock market reached dizzying heights in the 1990s, especially during the dot.com boom. Stock ownership spread through much of the population, with more than half of all U.S. households owning equities. Americans turned to the stock market to fund their retirements, their children's college educations, and other long-term aspirations. The emergence of online trading encouraged millionaire wannabes to try their hand at beating the market. Wall Street ads suggested that making money in the stock market was as easy as clicking a mouse. Take this ad starring Al the benevolent tow truck driver for Discover Brokerage. It aired at the height of the dot.com craze.

> PASSENGER: You invest online?
> DRIVER: Oh yeah, big time. Well, last few years anyway. I'm retired now.
> PASSENGER: You're retired?
> DRIVER: I don't need to do this—I just like helping people.
> PASSENGER: (Noticing a picture of an island) Vacation spot?
> DRIVER: Actually, it's a picture of my house.
> PASSENGER: It's an island.
> DRIVER: Well, technically it's a country. Weird thing about owning your own country, though, you have to name it.

Shades of the 1920s. Outrageous TV ads like this became emblems of the mass enthusiasm for stock speculation.

The market crashed in the spring of 2000 when investors fled stratospheric high-tech equity valuations. *Dot.com* became a reviled word. The market and the economy took another hit from the terrible tragedy of September 11, then stumbled along at an anemic pace, unable to rebound with any vigor from the 2001 recession. From the stock market's all-time high reached in March 2000 to its bottom in October 2002, more than $8.5 trillion in stock market wealth vaporized.[10] Nearly 3 million workers were handed pink slips during the downturn. And even when the major economic statistics such as gross domestic product (GDP) showed the economy recovering, business remained reluctant to add to payrolls. Bankruptcy filings by consumers soared to record levels in 2003. Bankruptcies in federal courts were up 98% since 1994.[11] The broad measures of business and consumer prices, such as the consumer price index, the producer price index, and the personal consumption deflator, were barely up, flat, or down. Deflation was in the air.

Pessimism is contagious when times are tough, neighbors are losing their jobs, and the Fed starts openly worrying about deflation. Author William Greider, with his typical deft touch, crystallized the underlying fear that surrounded the emergence of deflation:

> The United States is flirting with a low-grade
> depression, one that may last for years unless the
> government takes decisive action to overcome it. This
> would most likely be depression with a small d, not the
> financial collapse and "grapes of wrath" devastation
> Americans experienced during the Great Depression of
> the 1930s. . . . Depression means an economy that is
> stuck in a ditch and cannot get out, unable to regain its
> normal energies for expansion.[12]

Adding to the nightmare scenario, deflation wasn't just a historic artifact from the 1930s. In fact, there was a more recent and unsettling example: modern Japan's experience with deflation in recent years. And once again, the parallels to America in the 1920s and 1930s were ominous.

The island nation had been the world's economic juggernaut in the 1970s and 1980s. During those decades, Japan grew to become the world's second largest economy, and its export-oriented companies dominated everything from autos to steel to memory chips. This was the era of Japan as number one. Books like Paul Kennedy's *The Rise and Fall of the Great Powers* fed a gnawing fear that America would follow other imperial powers such as Austria–Hungary and Britain into economic decline. Japanese companies borrowed huge sums to expand their manufacturing operations at home and abroad. Japanese business titans splurged on everything from Van Gogh paintings to U.S. golf courses. Real estate values soared. The land beneath the Imperial Palace in Tokyo at one point was estimated to be worth more than all of California and, unbelievably, the real estate value of Japan greater than all the land in the United States. The stock market climbed to unimaginable heights.

American companies and government were exhorted to emulate the Japanese system or face an inevitable decline. The U.S. government should embrace Japanese mercantilism and forge close ties between government and business. Companies and banks should own each other. When author James Fallows shared a beer with an English friend in Tokyo in 1986, his friend said, "Why don't you just face the fact that you're second-raters, like us?" Masahiko Ishizuka, editor of the *Japan Economic Journal,* told Susan Chira of the *International Herald Tribune* in 1988, "You've been very slow in recognizing your decline. Now Japan and the United States are in a unique situation. . . . America's decline is the other side of the coin of Japan's rise."[13]

Bad forecast. The boom went bust in 1989. The stock and real estate markets collapsed, the financial system broke down as loans went bad, and the economy stagnated and declined during Japan's "lost decade" of the 1990s and early 2000s. The Imperial Palace was supposedly worth about half of Los Angeles. Residential real estate prices in 2002 were down about 80% from a dozen years before. Corporate bankruptcies had almost doubled over the same time period. The unemployment rate grimly marched to a post–World War II high. Wages and salaries declined by more than 4% between 1998 and 2003, and the major price indices were down between 4% and 9%. "Alan Greenspan is warning that deflation could hit the U.S.," wrote *Business Week* Tokyo bureau chief Brian Bremner in May 2003. "The European Central Bank is watching for telltale signs of price collapse in Germany. But in Japan, such warnings would be old news. Japan is already Deflation Nation and will be for years to come."[14]

The fear was that the dreaded "d" in Japan was a harbinger of what faced America. Indeed, Japan wasn't the only country mired in deflation. The International Monetary Fund calculated that episodes of falling consumer prices had increased from about 1% of countries in the first half of the 1990s to over 13% in the first three years of the millennium. A quarter of the world's 35 largest industrial and emerging markets were in deflation or showed inflation at less than 1%, including China, Singapore, Hong Kong, Taiwan, and Argentina. It was chilling to contemplate that America, Japan, and Germany—accounting for about half of the global economy—were in or near deflation.

THE SPREAD OF DEFLATION MEASURED BY THE CONSUMER PRICE INDEX

Percent of Countries Experiencing Deflation

	1991–96	1997–99	2000–02
All Countries	1.2	9.7	13.1
Industrial Countries	2.5	6.5	8.3
Emerging Countries	0.3	11.9	16.3

Data from the International Monetary Fund.

Depressions didn't stop with the 1930s. For instance, there were great depressions or unusually severe downturns in Argentina, Brazil, Mexico, and Chile in the 1980s. Banks failed. Workers were tossed out of jobs. Bankruptcies soared. Lenders foreclosed on homes and businesses. Social unrest mounted. These countries all suffered declines in economic activity comparable in magnitude to Canada, France, Germany, and the United States in the 1930s, according to University of Minnesota economists Edward Prescott and Timothy Kehoe in *Great Depressions of the Twentieth Century*.[15] Now, a depression is an economic calamity no matter how it is defined, but the word is carelessly tossed about during any economic downturn. So, here's the authors' definition of a great depression. They take the United States, the world's technological and economic leader, as their baseline. The long-term growth rate of the American economy measured as output per working person is 2% a year. So, a great depression is a sharp and huge deviation from this trend line—a drop of at least 20%. In their study, Prescott and Kehoe only included nations with a relatively modern economy. For example, their database includes Mexico but excludes Botswana. "The notion that the Great Depression is from the 1930s, and we don't have to worry about that now is wrong," says Kehoe.

America was also rocked by the worst business scandal since the 1930s. Back then, the public was shocked and disgusted by the self-dealing and shameless looting of corporate assets by scoundrels like Richard Whitney of the New York Stock Exchange and Charles Mitchell of National City Bank. Richard Whitney, acting president of the New York Stock Exchange during the crash and a famous broker with the prestigious firm J. P. Morgan as his client, symbolized Wall Street integrity in the 1920s. But he grandly lived well above his means. When insolvency loomed after the crash, he defrauded customers, his wife's trust fund, and the New York Yacht Club. He was caught, convicted, and sentenced to Sing-Sing prison. Charles Mitchell, known as "Sunshine Charley" and head of National City Bank, relentlessly pushed the salesmen in his financial supermarket, with branches in more than 50 cities, to peddle junk bonds and junk stocks to an unsuspecting public. He was forced to resign from National City Bank in 1933 and indicted for income tax evasion the following year, although he was later acquitted.[16] In the early 2000s, the malefactors of great wealth were unscrupulous characters like Kenneth Lay of Enron, who pocketed millions before his smoke-and-mirrors creation vanished wiping out investors and employees in 2002. Dennis Kozlowski of Tyco International tapped into company coffers to indulge in an orgy of spending that included a $6,000 shower curtain and a $2 million 40th birthday toga party for his wife in Sardinia. The appalling signs of ethical bankruptcy in executive suites, illegal practices on Wall Street, and corruption among accountants, lawyers, bankers, and other high-priced advisors wasn't a case of a few bad apples but signs of deep, systemic corruption among the commercial elite. CEOs at far too many companies around the turn of the millennium pocketed huge stock option gains while being less than forthright with shareholders about the state of the balance sheet—all the while claiming a divine right to gargantuan pay packages with no financial penalty for failure. The top management of the 25 largest corporate collapses in recent years pocketed some $3.3 billion in compensation, stock sales, payoffs, and other rewards even as their firms were heading into insolvency, according to calculations by the *Financial Times*.[17]

The deflation-and-depression scare even seeped into popular culture. The cartoon *Doonesbury* caught on to the deflation theme in 2003.[18]

> INTERVIEWER: Ari, any comment on the possibility
> that deflation might set in this year?
> ARI: Well, it's true that the economy's sluggish and the
> stock market is still in a hole, unemployment is up, and
> we're back to massive deficits.

Michael Silverstein, the self-styled Wall Street poet, penned an ode to deflation.[19]

> *Deflation's become*
> *The Fed's new concern,*

Prices are sinking
They say they discern.
But about this new thinking
I'm way out ahead,
In deflation's cold realm
I've long had to tread.

My whole life's deflated
It's lost its old puff,
What used to be easy
Has now gotten tough.
By a host of deep downturns
I have been beset,
The only thing rising
Is my credit debt.

I'll spare you the remaining stanzas, but you get the idea. It's a coincidence—but an intriguing one—that one of the block-buster movies in the summer of 2003 was about the depression-era racehorse Seabiscuit. Books like *Nickel and Dimed*, *White Collar Sweatshop*, and *Two-Income Trap* fed an end-of-era pessimism. The economic expansion and creative energies of the 1990s were long ago. For many, the 1990s seemed nothing more than a manic bubble, a dangerous false dawn exposed by an accounting scandal and a dot.com blowout. And now, to top it all off, deflation was a genuine risk. Growing segments of society were seized with what Mark Thornton, a senior fellow at the Ludwig von Mises Institute, calls *apoplithorismosphobia*, which is Greek for fear of deflation, or, perhaps more accurately, fear that deflation signaled a coming depression.[20] All of a sudden it no longer seemed unthinkable—albeit still a remote possibility—that the U.S. economy could slip into a vicious depression.

Alan Greenspan certainly seemed worried. A child of the depression growing up in the Washington Heights neighborhood of

New York City, the septuagenarian central banker, along with his Fed colleagues, peers in Europe and Britain, and monetary policy specialists, was unsettled by deflation. Fearful that the United States was on the verge of falling into a Japanese-style deflationary spiral, Greenspan opted for prudence and took out an insurance policy: The Fed cut its benchmark interest in the early summer of 2003, this time to 1%, the lowest level since 1958 when Dwight D. Eisenhower was president. The Fed launched a public relations campaign to shore up public confidence by sending governors across the country to give reassuring speeches about the extraordinary measures that the central bank could take to stave off deflation. The European Central Bank supported the Fed by cutting its rates and talked tough against deflation, especially with Germany's moribund economy on the cusp of deflation.

CHAPTER 2

TAPS ON THE SHOULDER

Money is the lifeblood of the nation.

—JONATHAN SWIFT

THE DEFLATION SCARE RECEDED TOWARD THE END of 2003. Management and workers had gone through a wrenching three years. Business had scaled back payrolls and growth prospects following the stock market bust, a recession and feeble recovery, and, most traumatically, terrorism and war. Companies had also overhauled operations, shored up balance sheets, and improved efficiency. The economy was finally expanding at a heady pace. Business investment picked up. Companies hired again. The fear that deflation signaled a looming depression either with a small d or a capital D—apoplithorismosphobia—faded. Deflation was so yesterday with economic activity picking up in both the United States and abroad.

Yet the deflation story isn't about depression. Deflation in the United States wasn't a temporary consequence of the bursting of the dot.com bubble and the 2000 to 2003 downturn. The recession amplified the powerful forces behind deflation, but the underlying trend won't disappear with strong sales and a low unemployment rate. Inflation is giving way to deflation. "The global economy is undergoing a remarkable structural transformation of a kind that occurs once every century or two," says Eisuke Sakakibara, Japan's former vice minister of finance known as "Mr. Yen" for his ability to move currency markets when in power. "The world is shifting from an era of structural inflation to one of deflation, in which prices for most manufactured goods and tradable services fall rather than rise."[1]

Right, I can just hear Wall Street veterans scoffing. They are fond of quoting the legendary investor John Templeton: "The four most expensive words in the English language are *this time it's different.*" They've been burned by too many new eras, new economies, and revolutionary transformations. After all, inflation is the economic condition we know. Baby boomers, for instance, are the inflation generation. It now takes some $945 to have the same purchasing power as $100 in 1946. Inflation is such an embedded part of our society that we all assume rising prices is the economy's natural state. The National Bureau of Economic Research (NBER) is a nonprofit organization based in Cambridge, Massachusetts. The NBER is the world's leading publisher of academic economic research through its *Working Paper* series, capitalism's little yellow pamphlets. A simple word search of the NBER *Working Paper* database for "inflation" and "deflation" turned up 491 articles on inflation compared to just 32 on deflation.

Many baby boomers and Wall Street traders remember when inflation reached double-digit levels in the 1970s, peaking at over 14% in 1980. Inflation was eventually contained through a combination of factors, including a tough anti-inflation battle waged by the Fed under the leadership of Paul Volcker and his successor, Alan Greenspan. The consumer price index averaged 7% in the '70s, 5.5% in the '80s, 3% in the '90s, and 2.5% in the early 2000s. The odds of another bout of double-digit 1970s-style inflation are remote. Still, economists routinely predict inflation will come back whenever growth is strong. Many executives see rising prices on the horizon, too, arguing that business costs will be propelled upward by government mandates and the deadweight costs of combating terrorism, such as installing more security cameras and hiring more guards at commercial office buildings. Even today people worry more about rising than falling prices. Here's a simple test. Ask a handful of colleagues at work about prices. Do the same thing with some neighbors. My guess is that most people will fret about higher prices except when it comes to high-tech gear like personal computers or digital cameras. "My health insurance premiums went up 40% this year," e-mailed a listener to *Sound Money*, my nationally syndicated public radio show. "And housing prices have almost doubled in this area in the past five years. Deflation?"

Yes, deflation. Of course, there will always be inflation scares and periodic spikes in the inflation rate. These episodes won't last long enough to turn persistent, however. The overall price level will lean toward stable to down. As Jack Welch, the legendary manager, told shareholders when he still ran General Electric: "Inflation has yielded to deflation as the shaping economic force."[2]

This Time Is Different

Every once in a great while the established economic order is overthrown. Within a span of decades, technological changes, organizational upheavals, and new ways of thinking transform economies. From the 1760s to the 1830s, steam engines, textile mills, and the Enlightenment produced the Industrial Revolution. The years 1880 to 1930 were shaped by the spread of electric power, mass production, and mass democracy. "Within a few short decades, society rearranges itself—its worldview; its basic values; its social and political structure; its arts; its key institutions," writes Peter Drucker, the management maestro. "Fifty years later, there is a new world. And the people born then cannot even imagine the world in which their grandparents lived and into which their own parents were born."[3]

Well, this time is different. Or maybe I should say, it's back to the future. From 1776 to 1965, America's overall price level was essentially flat. Inflationary flare-ups were mostly associated with major wars until the post–World War II era. These inflationary conflagrations were quickly extinguished in the aftermath of war. Stable to falling prices dominated the rest of the time, especially in the latter part of the 19th century, the last time there was a tightly integrated global economy.

It's sometimes obvious when a historic divide is crossed. The 1929 stock market crash. The 1973 oil shock. Far more often, "change creeps upon us incrementally, punctuated by upheavals that, often as not, are rationalized as part of business as usual," said the late legendary financier Leon Levy. "Only later do we realize that the world has been turned on its head."[4] Levy called these events "a tap on the shoulder." Deflation may have taken a lot of people by surprise in 2003, but the price trend didn't emerge overnight. It had been building for years, a secular undertow to all the cyclical twists and turns in the economy. There were many deflation taps on the shoulder.

The first tap to emphasize is the most significant: the appointment of Paul Volcker as chairman of the Federal Reserve in 1979. Inflation had spiraled out of control in the 1970s, with prices climbing at the pump, the supermarket, and the furniture store. Government campaigns against inflation had failed miserably, such as Richard Nixon's wage and price controls and Gerald Ford's "Whip Inflation Now" buttons. Nothing seemed to work at stemming the inflationary tide. The public had learned to anticipate that prices would always go higher. The consumers' motto became buy now, and borrow lots of money.

Where was the Fed? There had been no serious, sustained effort to break the inflation spiral under the leadership of Fed chairmen Arthur Burns and G. William Miller. President Jimmy Carter had appointed Miller, the chief executive of Textron, to head up the Fed. While the Nixon appointee, Burns, ran a disastrous monetary policy during his tenure at the Fed, Miller got much of the blame, since inflation skyrocketed under his watch. Eventually, Carter shuffled the inept Miller out of the Fed and named him secretary of the Treasury. Carter replaced Miller with Paul Volcker, an imposing, abrasive, six-foot-seven president of the Federal Reserve Bank of New York. Volcker was a central banker steeped in the ideology that inflation was the economy's number one problem—and that the job of the Fed was to eliminate it. He stomped on the monetary brakes, sending the economy into two recessions. Millions of workers lost their jobs, companies went out of business across the country, but the process of containing inflation had begun. Volcker was followed by another inflation hawk, Alan Greenspan.

Another tap worth highlighting came when Wal-Mart, the Bentonville, Arkansas, discounter, became the world's largest retailer in 1992. Retailing has never been the same since Wal-Mart founder Sam Walton created a company dedicated to relentlessly squeezing its suppliers and manufacturers to cut prices, then passing those savings on to consumers with its "everyday low price" strategy. Of course, there had always been relatively well-off consumers who pursued bargain hunting as sport, as well as low-income families who shopped in cut-rate stores out of necessity. Today, all consumers expect low prices as they flock to discount retailers like Target, Home Depot, Costco, Office Depot, Walgreen's, and so on. Wal-Mart, the world's largest retailer and America's largest private employer, saves its U.S. customers an estimated $100 billion annually by wringing cost inefficiencies out of the retail supply chain and by forcing competitors to match its low prices.[5] Wal-Mart is a major force behind the inflation's demise. "Economists now credit the company's Everyday Low Prices with contributing to Everyday Low Inflation, meaning that all Americans," writes journalist Jerry Useem, "unknowingly benefit from the retailer's clout."[6]

The next tap was generated by Japan. Japan, the second largest economy in the world, sank into a deflationary stupor in the 1990s. Yet most everyone in the West except specialists ignored Japan's bout with deflation. A falling price level in Japan was considered a special case—the result of an unusually inept central bank, an ossified political culture, and a bankrupt banking system—rather than a harbinger that deflation was coming out of its six-decade slumber. To Westerners, Japan was unique when its distinct brand of mercantile capitalism seemed unbeatable in the 1980s. In the late 1990s it remained distinctive, the deflation nation.

No one missed the next tap, although the deflationary significance of the Internet is still underappreciated. The Internet industry was born in August 1995, with the wildly successful initial public offering (IPO) of Netscape Communications Corporation at $28 a share, peaking at $75 per share before closing at $58. Netscape didn't invent the first Internet browser, but its version was easy to navigate compared to its competitors. The Netscape IPO showed financiers from Sand Hill Road in Silicon Valley to the corner of Wall Street and Broad in Manhattan that a bright commercial future beckoned online. The dot.com boom followed. Like electricity, the railroads, and other great inventions, the Internet and information technologies would transform the way we live and work. Ebay.com. Amazon. com. Mayoclinic.org. Census.gov. Think about it. Without leaving our desks at work or at home, millions and millions of us log on and e-mail friends, shop for books, sell aging vinyl albums, read the latest research on global warming, watch a press conference, send files to colleagues, and print out a barbecue recipe from a restaurant we visited while on vacation years ago.

The Internet is an inherently deflationary technology. The Internet makes it easy for consumers and businesses to shop for the lowest possible price. Entrepreneurs with a good idea and high bandwidth can attract customers and challenge established industry players. For instance, the airline and hotel industries have lost pricing power in recent years to corporate and individual customers who go online to Expedia, Travelocity, Hotwire, and other cyberportals seeking deals. Downloading, legal or illegal, undermined the music industry's strategy of keeping CD prices high. Companies such as Apple Computer and Dell have developed products to sell music cheaply online. The movie business is next.

Even more important, the Internet is a critical technology for slashing costs and boosting productivity. Drug company researchers collaborate around the globe using the Internet. Automakers are installing Wi-Fi devices in their plants to track inventory and speed production. The Internet makes it easier than ever for U.S. companies to outsource manufacturing production to China and brainpower work to India. "The Internet builds bridges between low-cost economies and high-cost economies and allows arbitrage to take place," says Mohan Sawhney, professor of technology at Kellogg Graduate School of Management at Northwestern University. "It will level pricing differentials and costs. It will reduce costs around the world."

Asia's economic and financial problems in the late 1990s signaled a shift in the global fundamentals toward deflation. This was no tap. It was more like a roundhouse punch. The abrupt devaluation of the Thai bath in 1997 set off a currency, stock, and bond market collapse throughout much of Asia. The shock reverberated to all corners of the globe, revealing a global excess of capacity to produce all manner of goods and services.

The Asian experience of the past half century marked the greatest economic transformations in history. Asia's emerging markets were technologically backward, dirt-poor economies at the end of World War II. The World Bank famously—or perhaps infamously—forecast in 1960 that over the next 40 years economic growth in sub-Saharan Africa—with its more educated population and rich commodity resources—would soar. The export-dependent economies of Asia would stagnate. Instead, Korea, Hong Kong, Singapore, Taiwan, Indonesia, Malaysia, and Thailand grew rapidly, while sub-Saharan Africa languished. East Asia's economies became relatively modern, competitive economies within a span of decades.

But success bred excess. East Asian companies went on a building binge financed by plenty of low-cost government money, much of it targeted toward favored companies. Imagine, East Asia accounted for about half the growth in world output in the 1990s. A fierce battle for markets broke out as hundreds of thousands of new factories churned out cars, chemicals, mobile phones, textiles, computer chips, electronic gizmos, and other products for world markets. The massive scale and increasing sophistication of production in South Korea, Malaysia, Indonesia, Singapore, Taiwan, and elsewhere in Asia washed over the global economy, driving prices ever lower. Yet Asian companies earned so little—if anything—on their sales that even the slightest downturn or financial disturbance made meeting their enormous debt burdens onerous. When those loans soured, these economies foundered as investor confidence faltered. Still, to avoid massive layoffs, exporting companies cut prices to maintain sales, exacerbating global deflationary pressures.

Around this time a minority of American executives, deeply aware of relentless international competition and fearful of the competitive threat posed by the 'Net, started worrying about deflation. For instance, Jack Welch, then head of General Electric and the nation's most admired CEO, argued vociferously that management needed to change its strategy and tactics. He was determined to remold GE so that it could thrive in a deflationary environment. "The one unacceptable comment from a GE leader in '98 will be 'Prices are lower than we thought, and we couldn't get costs out fast enough to make our commitments,'" said Welch. "Unacceptable behavior, because prices will be lower than you're planning, so you better start taking action this week."[7]

Welch wasn't alone in his deflation forecast. A reading of the minutes from the December 1997 Federal Market Open Committee meeting shows that deflation was a frequent topic among business audiences. For instance, Edward G. Boehne, head of the Federal Reserve Bank of Philadelphia, noted that as a good central banker he always talked about the dangers of inflation before audiences. Yet the first question he found himself fielding was always about deflation. "In my view, this deflation talk is not something one can just dismiss," said Boehne. "In part, I believe these comments are reflecting the fierce competition that businesses face, and they also reflect the fact that most businesses find deflation harmful." Still, most economists dismissed the deflation concern gaining currency among CEOs. Take the response of Alice Rivlin, the Fed's vice chairman, at the same meeting. She was "mystified by the deflation question that we get every time we make a speech. The prospect that prices actually will go down in the face of what we normally see as continuing strength in the economy strikes me as bizarre."[8]

Perhaps Fed chairman Alan Greenspan didn't quite agree with his vice chairman. That's one way to read the next tap. Greenspan spoke at the 1998 American Economics Association annual meeting. It's a professional gathering of some 9,000 economists, ranging from the profession's leading lights to newly minted Ph.D.s looking for a job. Greenspan's topic: "The Problems of Price Measurement." It was hardly the kind of title or talk to grab widespread attention. Not many people really cared about empirical research suggesting the official price measures, such as the consumer price index, overstate the rate of inflation. Inflation around the world had dropped significantly. Greenspan wondered during his talk whether the odds of deflation were unexpectedly high now that inflation rates were so low in the major industrial nations. "Indeed, some observers have begun to question whether deflation is now a possibility and to assess the potential difficulties such a development might pose for the economy," said Greenspan.[9]

Two more significant events deserve notice, both involving transformations in the global economy. First, China joined the World Trade Organization in late 2001. China is a center of global manufacturing attracting enormous sums of foreign investment. The Asian giant is a major player in labor-intensive manufacturing such as textiles and apparel. Take a walk through any retail store and look at the labels—many say "Made in China." The stamp is even more prevalent in toy stores. Chinese manufacturers are rapidly moving up the value-added chain, making such high-tech products as digital cameras, cell phones, camcorders, televisions, personal computers, and cars. China's share of Asia's total electronics export market has more than doubled over five years to 30% in 2002. Its bilateral trade surplus with the United States has roughly doubled since 1997, to more than $100 billion. Simply put, highly competitive Chinese factories are exporting deflation by putting competitive price pressure on manufacturers everywhere else. The impact of China on global economic activity will only increase over the next several decades.

Second, American companies are outsourcing white-collar and skilled service-sector jobs overseas, especially to India. Factory and blue-collar jobs had been disappearing for a quarter century as overseas competition forced Smokestack America to restructure its operations—lay off workers, invest in new technologies, consolidate operations, and open plants in low-cost countries. The trend accelerated during the 2000–2003 downturn. Now brainpower jobs are going offshore. A major reason is that the Internet makes it easy to work with well-educated cheap foreign labor. Forrester Research, the consulting firm, has estimated the United States will lose some three million service jobs in programming, engineering, accounting, and the like to India, China, the Philippines, and other developing nations by 2015—almost 4,000 a week. The cost in lost wages? $136 billion. "The white-collar worker is about to go through what the blue-collar worker went through in the 1970s," says Paul Saffo, research director at the Institute for the Future. "In the global society, no job touched by a computer or a telephone will be secure. It's inevitable that a significant portion of jobs will go overseas."

India and China accounted for an estimated 45% of the world economy in the early 19th century. Once again, both giant nations are making their presence known, China as a manufacturing hub and India as a high-tech base. Both nations also have a large diaspora around the world, offering money and talent to their former homelands, since both have now abandoned the socialist model of economic development for capitalism. A research report by economists at Goldman Sachs estimates that in fewer than 40 years, the combined economies of China, India, Russia, and Brazil could be bigger than the United States, Japan, Germany, the United Kingdom, Italy, and France (in dollar terms).[10] Deflation is the natural state during an era of expanding markets and technological innovation.

Taken altogether, this time *is* different.

CHAPTER 3

THE SUPPLY-SIDE ECONOMY

[T]he essential point to grasp is that in
dealing with capitalism, we are dealing with
an evolutionary process. . . . Capitalism,
then, is by nature a form or method of
economic change and not only never is, but
never can be, stationary.

—JOSEPH SCHUMPETER

 ONE OF THE SAVVIEST BUSINESSMEN I KNOW, A shrewd deal maker with plenty of experience at home and abroad, gave me a quizzical look over the remains of lunch. "So, you think there's going to be deflation?" he asked. "Yes, I do," I replied. "Well, I think you're nuts," he said, smiling. "The economy is coming back."

He was right. That is, about the economy. The rebound was apparent when we met sometime early in the fall of 2003. But you could say that our divergence of opinion about the prospect for deflation began on October 29, 1929. The stock market crash popularly marks the start of the Great Depression, and memories of that terrible time have permanently linked financial calamity, economic disaster, and deflation. But the conventional notion that a persistent decline in prices is always a disaster, an economic disease to be avoided at all costs, a depression in the making, is wrong. University of Minnesota economist Timothy Kehoe examined the record of deflation in 15 countries over 100 years. There were indeed a number of episodes when nations experienced both deflation and depression. But it was more common for economies to grow during periods of deflation. "I see essentially no empirical link between deflation and depression," says Kehoe.[1] Economists Michael D. Bordo and Angela Redish agree with that conclusion in a fascinating paper that carefully distinguishes between good and bad episodes of deflation. "Deflation has had a 'bad rap,' " say Bordo and Redish.[2]

The historic record is clear: Hyperdeflation, say a 1930s deflation rate of 5% to 10%, is ruinous. Period. The record is mixed when it comes to mild deflation, say a rate of 1% to 2% a year. Sometimes mild deflation signals a vigorous, healthy economy. What matters is why are overall prices persistently falling, say Bordo and Redish. Bad deflation stems from a "demand shock," perhaps a bankrupt banking system, a collapse in the money supply, or some other trauma that pushes an economy into a downward deflationary spiral. Good deflation can coexist with strong economic growth when the primary cause is a "supply shock" coming from a string of major technological innovations that push costs and prices down, strong productivity improvements, consumer and business gains from freer international trade, and the like. "Such benign productivity-driven deflation was a common occurrence during the last part of the 19th century, when people routinely looked forward to goods getting cheaper," says George Selgin, an economist at the University of Georgia.[3]

By the way, a focus on the economy's supply side has little to do with the "tax cuts will pay for themselves" nonsensical mantra of Steve Forbes, Jude Wanniski, the *Wall Street Journal* editorial page, and other modern-day tax-cut zealots. Yes, taxes on income and capital do affect long-term incentives to work and invest. But most professional economists look on the simplistic supply-side economics with disdain. As the astute financial journalist David Warsh put it, supply siders insist on "peddling a grotesque caricature of Keynesian doctrine in which tax cuts rather than deficit spending are continually necessary to prod an otherwise stagnant economy, proclaiming at every stage the medicine was working"—no matter that the deficit reduction program of President Clinton, which included some tax increases, helped set the stage for the nation's longest economic expansion.[4]

A more traditional approach toward supply-side economics includes the impact of technological innovation, changes in production, advances in business organization, immigration and trade flows, and the education level of the workforce. Take the expansion of 1991 to 2001. Yes, taxes were raised on upper-income families. But the American economy benefited from a real supply-side revolution. The productive capacity of business rose sharply as huge investments in high-tech gear paid off. More than a million immigrants a year came to the United States, supplying vital brainpower and technical talent and filling low-wage jobs. The labor force was better educated than previous generations, with about half the adult population having at least some college education, up sharply from 40% in 1991 and a third in 1982.[5] Money poured into the capital markets, with the mutual fund assets surging from $1 trillion in 1990 to $6.9 trillion in 2000 and the number of households owning mutual funds doubling to 52 million. Knowledge and information were disseminated to the far corners of the globe over the Internet. Entrepreneurship flourished, with young people eager to start their own companies and restless executives leaving established companies for fledgling start-ups.

During the long expansion the consumer price index fell from 3.1% in 1991 to 1.6% in 2001.

Supply-Side Deflation

You have to go back to the 1800s to find examples of persistent deflation, especially in the late 19th century. Like now, the latter part of
the 19th century and the early years of the 20th century were defined
by the rapid emergence of an integrated world economy. Deflation
was the dominant price trend. Yet for much of the pre-1914 world
economy, sustained periods of deflation were not associated with
depression. The late 1800s were largely a time of prosperity and peace
that ended with the violent outbreak of World War I. To be sure,
plenty of battles and wars were fought on the periphery of the global
economy in the 1800s as the major industrial nations pursued their
imperial ambitions in Africa, Asia, and Latin America. Europe's balance of power system, aided by a largely isolationist America, managed to contain the economic and financial damage from colonial
conflicts while the race for spheres of influence accelerated the
expansion of the world economy. "Despite recurrent financial turbu-
lence, the period between the end of the American Civil War and the
outbreak of World War I was marked by a mighty force of economic
growth and industrialization in both America and Europe," writes
Peter Bernstein in *The Power of Gold*. "Peace helped, too: no major
wars were fought within Europe from 1870 to 1914, while the only
military activity to engage the United States was the Spanish-
American War of 1898."[6]

Great Britain was the dynamic center of the industrial world.
Britain had come to embrace free trade policies, and traditional
mercantilist trade barriers fell. International trade flourished. The
volume of world foreign trade per capita was more than 25 times
greater at the end than at the beginning of the 19th century. Vast
amounts of capital flowed across borders. A lot of the money was
invested in high-risk ventures such as building railroad and communication networks. By 1913, the share of foreign securities traded in
London was 59% of all traded securities; and by 1914, the stock of

foreign direct investment had reached $14 billion, or one-third of world foreign investment. British foreign assets were equivalent to 150% of its domestic economy. The comparable figures for Germany, France, and the United States were 40%, 15%, and 10%, respectively.[7]

Immigrants crossed borders and oceans in astonishing numbers. Some 17.5 million people left Europe behind to seek their fortune, about two-thirds of them relocating to America. A large number of Chinese and Indian workers labored in plantations and mines, as well as taking advantage of entrepreneurial opportunities opening up in Burma, Indonesia, Malaysia, and elsewhere in Southeast Asia. New technologies and industries in Europe and America like electric power, the railroad, petroleum, steel, telegraph, and pharmaceuticals transformed work and the rhythm of everyday life.[8] An eloquent passage in the 1848 Communist Manifesto by Karl Marx and Friedrich Engels captured the era:

> The bourgeoisie, during its rule of scarce one hundred
> years, has created more massive and more colossal
> productive forces than have all preceding generations
> together. Subjection of nature's forces to man,
> machinery, application of chemistry to industry and
> agriculture, steam navigation, railways, electric
> telegraphs, clearing of whole continents for cultivation,
> canalization or rivers, whole populations conjured out of
> the ground—what earlier century had even a
> presentiment that such productive forces slumbered in
> the lap of social labor?[9]

This was also the era of the international gold standard, the mythical monetary system that defined the global economy of the 19th century. Economists still look back on the classic gold standard with nostalgia because it promoted international price stability. A shared belief—a commitment to the economic and political benefits of the gold anchor—facilitated international commerce and investment. A shortage of gold relative to the dramatic increase in international economic activity gave a deflationary bias to the world economy—that is, overall prices fell.

Britain was a charter member of the gold club. Most other nations in the early 1800s still backed their currencies with silver or both silver and gold (bimetallism). The rush to embrace gold came in the 1870s when America, Germany, France, Scandinavian countries, and a number of other European countries backed their currency with the ancient metal. Gold, a trusted store of wealth, gave entrepreneurs confidence in the value of currencies. It was also a check on government profligacy, a historical willingness of government leaders to debase the currency to raise tax revenues or fund foreign adventures on the cheap. David Ricardo, the 19th-century British economist, expressed a widespread sentiment by writing that "neither a State nor a bank ever has had the unrestricted power of issuing paper money, without abusing that power; in all states, therefore, the issue of paper money ought to be under some check and control; and none seems so proper as that of subjecting the issuers of paper money to the obligation of paying their notes, either in gold coin or in bullion." [10]

The value of national currencies was set in relationship to a fixed weight of gold, making it easy for business to exchange monies across borders. Entrepreneurs could expand overseas without worrying about foreign exchange risk that would erase profits. (Whether the business ventures themselves made money was a different matter.) Governments were committed—and it is the commitment that is key—to convert their currency if asked into gold. Signs of inflation or some other mismanagement would cause a flight of gold, forcing central banks or treasuries to hike interest rates and take other defensive measures to restore fiscal and monetary probity. The cost of subordinating domestic economic policy to international monetary stability was high on workers, farmers, and many other sectors of society, however. This was an era of laissez-faire, free markets, small governments, and monetary stability. There was no safety net for those who lost their job or for farmers and entrepreneurs driven out of business by the dictates of the international gold standard. Nevertheless, the core countries of the developed world grew wealthy off the unprecedented levels of trade and investment supported by the gold standard.

The gold standard contributed to the sustained deflation experienced by members of the international monetary order. The quantity theory of money, an approach to the price level developed by David Hume, the Scottish philosopher and friend of Adam Smith, holds that changes in the quantity of money are the main force behind inflation and deflation. Now called monetarism, the theory argues that inflation is caused by rapid increases in the quantity or supply of money. For instance, inflation took hold in Europe with the vast inflow of gold and silver from the Americas in the 16th century. On the other hand, deflation stems from the decline or too slow increase in the money supply. In the latter part of the 19th century, the world production of gold remained fairly constant. But economic output in Britain, the United States, Canada, and other industrializing nations grew fast during a period of rapid technological innovation. Too little money was chasing too many goods. The demand for gold also increased as more nations joined the gold club. It wasn't until the gold supply expanded following new discoveries in South Africa, Australia, and the Americas that price pressures eased and inflation became the dominant price trend. All economists are monetarists now in the sense that everyone agrees that money matters, and that changes in the gold supply did affect the price level in the 19th century. Nevertheless, while the gold standard was a major factor behind deflation, the fall in the general price level in an era of rapid economic growth and increasing international trade seems to reflect more the structural impact of a telecommunications, distribution, and production revolution.

Take Britain's experience. British prices fell at an average annual rate of 0.8% between 1875 and 1896. Economic historians once referred to this period as the "great depression." But that phrase is highly misleading, to say the least. Perhaps it should have been called the great deflation, as British business struggled to cope with declining prices over a quarter of a century. The gloom was understandable. British leaders watched the rapid rise of the American and German economies. Worried about their nation's declining industrial competitiveness, troubled elites devoured books like *Made in Germany* and *The American Invasion*[11]—in the 1980s American elites would fret over declining U.S. international competitiveness compared to Japan, the Asian Tigers, Germany, and much of Europe. Yet, as the leading British economist Alfred Marshall reported to the Parliamentary Gold and Silver Commission in 1887, the decline in prices wasn't a sign of chronic depression in either economic output or employment. Quite the contrary, since worker wages and living standards rose, the price pressure on profits didn't curb investment, and technological innovation accounted for much of the price decline. The gold standard contributed to deflation, but the impact of technology and trade was more significant for the economic condition of a falling price level.

> *Alfred Marshall:* Now, I do not think there has been any period in which there have been so many great changes. . . . The changes are, I think, chiefly due to the great fall, the unparalleled fall, in the cost of transport, which renders it worth while to do a great many things that it was not worth while to do before; but besides this there are an immense number of changes in all industries, chemical and mechanical. . . .
>
> *Mr. Barbour:* You said that in so far as the fall in prices had tended to give the wage-earning classes more for their labor, it was a distinct gain?
>
> *Alfred Marshall:* That is my opinion.[12]

Eric Hobsbawm, the great historian of the industrial era, agrees that the defining attribute of the period was falling prices. He marks 1870 as a distinct turning point for Britain's working class—and for the better. Worker wages were one-third higher in 1900 than in 1875 and 84% greater than in 1850. Living standards improved, especially since working families benefited from cheap imported food and falling prices for goods. Meat consumption per head shot up by almost a third. Fruit, long a luxury only the wealthy could afford, was consumed by the masses. Lower prices made it profitable for entrepreneurs to set up retail shops in working-class neighborhoods. Prices for innovations like sewing machines and bicycles came down fast, and by the turn of the century consumer goods like these were commonplace. "In a word, between 1870 and 1900 the pattern of British working class life which writers, dramatists, and TV producers of the 1950s thought of as 'traditional' came into being," writes Hobsbawm. "It was not 'traditional' then, but new."[13]

A similar tale unfolded for the United States, only more so. Deflation and better everyday circumstances went together. The wholesale price level fell about 1.5% annually between 1870 and 1900. Living standards improved as real incomes (that is, income after taking inflation into account) rose by 85%, or about 5% a year.[14] Put somewhat differently, in 1900 it took only $100 to have the same purchasing power as $155 in 1870. (That's a stunning outcome, considering we are used to a very different result over the past thirty years: $100 in 1973 is worth less than $25 thirty years later.) The U.S. economy grew threefold as America went from an agricultural republic to an industrial empire. Farming and ranching were the main generators of income until the 1880s. By 1900, the annual value of manufacturers was more than twice that of agriculture. In the 1860s, right after the end of the Civil War, America's industrial output lagged behind Germany, France, and Great Britain. By 1900, America had become the world's leading industrial power with a combined output greater than its main European rivals.

One way to grasp the transformation is to look at how life changed for Marshall Wyatt Earp. He fought the legendary shootout at OK Corral in the cow town of Tombstone, Arizona, in 1881. Horses and horse-drawn carriages were common, the railroad the main link between regions, indoor plumbing rare, and the frontier beckoned. Earp died in Los Angeles in 1929. The city teemed with cars, electricity, indoor plumbing, radio, and television. He lived off income from his mining and real estate investments, rubbed shoulders with Hollywood actor friends, and was an advisor on silent film westerns.[15] "The last three decades of the century witnessed extraordinary growth in industrial (and agricultural) production, the creation of an American industrial heartland, the rise of the corporation and new ways of conducting business, and the appearance of startling new technologies: few could imagine in 1875 the world of telephones, electrical lighting, steel-beamed skyscrapers, and even cars with gasoline engines that had emerged by 1900," summarizes historian Walter Licht in *Industrializing America*.[16]

Again, the international gold standard was a force for deflation. But the supply side of the economy, including trade, technology, business organization, and immigration, also put enormous downward pressure on prices. The United States was a common domestic market with relatively few barriers to trade and commerce. Ruthless entrepreneurs and financiers like Andrew Carnegie, John D. Rockefeller, J. P. Morgan, and other robber barons or prospering fathers, depending on your point of view, created a new form of capitalism dominated by the modern business enterprise. Alfred Chandler Jr., the dean of business historians, emphasizes how these entrepreneurs eventually exploited the productivity of mass production through a three-pronged costly investment: (1) build large factories, (2) create national and international distribution networks, and (3) hire professional management.[17]

The economic impact was dramatic. For instance, in 1870 Britain forged more steel than the rest of the world combined. Three decades later, the United States was producing twice as much steel as Britain—much of it from the mills of Andrew Carnegie. Here's how Harvard Business School professor Richard Tedlow describes Andrew Carnegie's business philosophy. "Hire the best engineers to design the plants. Spend what needs to be spent to keep operating costs low. Only the slimmest margins were necessary, and in fact only they were desirable. The lower the margins, the lower the price. The lower the price, the larger the market. The larger the market, the greater the scale economies. The greater the scale economies, the greater the competitive advantage."[18]

The unprecedented productivity of big business helped drive prices lower. By 1896, wholesale prices were only 47% of their 1869 level. The largely benign decline reflected forces operating on the supply side of the market. "In cases of supply-induced deflation, cost changes lead price changes. Changing technology and discovery in an economy are necessary conditions for cost-induced deflation," writes George Edward Dickey in *Money, Prices, and Growth: The American Experience, 1869–1896.* "Business profits would be maintained or enhanced and output could continue to advance without any constraint other than that imposed by full employment. Deflation in this case is a direct result of the rapid growth of output and is not an inhibitor to growth. . . . The nineteenth century American experience demonstrated that economic growth is compatible with deflation."[19]

What about stock and bond returns? Stocks returned an average of 8.5% a year and bonds 6.6% from 1870 to 1900. Hardly a disastrous return on investment considering that the long-term return on stocks has averaged 7% and bonds 3.5% since 1802, according to data compiled by Jeremy Siegel, professor of finance at the Wharton School.[20]

China's Deflation

The combination of deflation and fast economic growth didn't disappear along with the gold standard and Victorian corsets. No, China is a contemporary example of productivity-driven deflation. Japan's deflationary stagnation is attracting all the attention and

A TALE OF TWO DEFLATIONS

Percent Change, 1990–2002

	JAPAN		CHINA	
	ECONOMIC GROWTH*	CONSUMER PRICE INDEX	ECONOMIC GROWTH*	CONSUMER PRICE INDEX
1990	5.2	3.1	4.2	2.1
1991	3.3	3.3	9.1	3.0
1992	0.9	1.7	14.1	5.3
1993	0.4	1.3	13.1	13.0
1994	1.0	0.7	12.6	21.7
1995	1.9	−0.1	9.0	14.8
1996	3.6	0.1	9.8	6.1
1997	1.8	1.7	8.6	0.7
1998	−1.2	0.7	7.8	−2.5
1999	0.2	−0.3	7.2	−3.0
2000	2.1	−0.7	8.4	−1.5
2001	0.8	−0.8	7.0	−0.8
2002	0.6	−0.9	8.0	−1.3

*Gross domestic product, adjusted for inflation.

Data from the Federal Reserve Bank of Cleveland and the Federal Reserve Bank of Minneapolis.

worry. It's less appreciated that prices have been falling in China, the world's most dynamic economy. The People's Republic of China has been growing at an astonishing 6% to 8% annual pace in recent years. Prices have been declining in the world's sixth largest economy at an average annual rate of less than 2% since 1998.

What is causing lower prices in China? A monumental shift away from a state-dominated system that wasted vast resources to a far more efficient market economy. The Chinese central bank has been running a tight money policy to keep inflation at bay. And since China has abandoned autarchy to become one of the world's largest trading economies, fierce competition from neighboring countries is also keeping a lid on the prices of tradable goods. Perhaps the most telling observation of China's remarkable economic journey comes from Jagdish Bhagwati, a leading international economist at Columbia University. China pursued autarchic economic policies, extreme government intervention and controls, as well as a proliferation of an inefficient public sector from 1950 to 1980. China's economy suffered from weak growth during those three decades, and the incidence of poverty in 1978 was 28%. Over the next two decades, however, China increasingly integrated into the world economy, growth picked up, and by 2000 the poverty rate had plunged to 9%.[21]

Certainly, companies headquartered in the major industrial nations aren't acting as if China is a deflationary basket case. The combination of rising wealth, increased industrial sophistication, and the promise of continuing market-friendly reform have persuaded multinational corporations to pour billions into the Asian giant. Foreign direct investment in China totaled some $430 billion between 1994 and 2003, with much of that sum coming in the last couple of years. U.S. multinational corporations in China had 13,600 employees in 1990 with sales of $775 million. By 2002, the number of employees had swelled to 537,000 and sales had expanded to $61 billion.[22] China is no longer just a giant factory producing cheap goods for the rest of the world. It is a fast-growing consumer market. Rising incomes and wide-open competition allow Chinese households to improve the quality of everyday life. China is going middle class.

For example, at the end of 1998, China had 24 million mobile phone subscribers; by early 2003 that figure had mushroomed to 226 million. China is the fourth largest auto market in the world, after America, Japan, and Germany. Merrill Lynch notes that companies like Unilever, Procter & Gamble, and Danone are budgeting for price deflation of 5% to 10% a year in China, but since they expect sales volume to double every year, these companies will be able to maintain operating margins of 10% to 12% annually.[23] "China is not just a source of lower prices but an engine of world growth," says Paul Laudicina, vice president and managing director of A. T. Kearney's Global Business Policy Council. "As we look at the world now, by 2015 the global economy will be dominated by China and the United States."

CHAPTER 4

DEFLATION,
AMERICAN STYLE

All of the evidence suggests that in fact the
American deflation was essentially the result
of shifting supply conditions which
permitted prices to be pulled rather than
pushed down: Output typically increased
when prices fell, relative prices generally fell
with money prices, and profits grew. Supply
rather than demand forces thus dominated
price movements in individual product
markets. Rapid growth continued in spite of
falling prices which were generated by rising
output. The growing money supply generally
prevented demand forces from dominating
price movements and thus slowing the
growth process.

—EDWARD DICKEY

WELL, WHAT ABOUT THE UNITED STATES? THE
deflation scare hit during an unusual economic
downturn, the tenth recession of the post–World
War II era. No two recessions are the same.
Economists are divided about whether the Fed

follows the business cycle or manages the big swings in economic activity. Still, there is a basic rhythm to downturns over the past half century—a demand-side recession as consumer spending falls sharply. Inflation is stirring, so the Fed raises interest rates to dampen shopping at the mall, the car dealership, and the developer lot. Business contracts with the drop in consumer spending. Companies lay off workers. Spending falls. Inflation pressures ease. Now, the Fed doesn't actually want a recession. But the central bank, along with other economists, is slow to realize the downturn has gone too far. The Fed then gives the economy some relief by loosening the reins of monetary policy. Interest rates come down, consumer buying picks up, business starts hiring, and the pace of activity accelerates.

The 2001 downturn was largely a supply-side recession. Inflation was dormant. Greenspan did hike rates in 2000 to tap on the economic brakes. But the primary reason for the downturn was a vicious hangover from a high-tech investment binge that went on too long. Companies were saddled with excess capacity that started eating into earnings, and the stock market cratered as the profit outlook deteriorated. The shock of the market's cataclysmic decline forced companies to pull back sharply. The tragedy of 9/11 further dampened activity. So did the march toward war in Afghanistan and Iraq. Managers struggled to maintain profitability by canceling investment plans, laying off workers, exporting jobs and tasks to cheaper regions of the world, all with an eye toward restoring profits. With the overall consumer and producer price indices so low, and with a number of industries and services experiencing steep price declines, the risk of deflation mounted. Haunted by the deflationary experience of Japan, the Fed aggressively cut rates. During the 2001 downturn, consumer spending remained a bright spot. The lowest rates in four decades encouraged people to buy homes, cars, and other big-ticket items.

Of course, the recovery finally gained momentum. The Fed and Wall Street greeted the news with relief. It was time to start worrying about prospects for inflation rather than deflation, a much more familiar and therefore comforting topic. But over the long haul, deflation is here to stay.

The Secular Undertow of Deflation

Indeed, deflation is desirable as the economy regains its vigor. As in 19th-century America, deflation today reflects fundamental changes on the economy's supply side set in motion about a quarter century ago—supply-side forces that have converged, reinforced one another, and gained energy over the years. At the same time, a new international monetary system has evolved that contains a bias toward lower prices. Deflation itself is a cause of change. Deflation, like inflation before it, is taking on a momentum of its own. "Of all the recording devices that can reveal to a historian the fundamental movements of an economy, monetary phenomena are without doubt the most sensitive," wrote the French historian Marc Bloch. "But to recognize their importance as symptoms would do them less than full justice. They have been and are, in their turn, causes. They are something like a seismograph, which not only measure the movements of the earth but sometimes provokes them."[1]

Look at the issue this way. When I broke into journalism I covered the markets. My boss was Jeffrey Madrick, a brilliant journalist and editor. Like a good editor, he took me out to lunch to talk about his perspective on reporting on the markets. A lot of what you read or hear about why the market went up or down is nonsense, he said. It may be well-written nonsense. It may be entertaining nonsense. But it is nonsense nevertheless. Fact is, hedge funds, mutual funds, individual investors, insurance companies, Wall Street investment banks, and overseas investors buy and sell stocks for many reasons. On any given day no one really knows why the stock market goes up or down. Still, said Madrick, the information isn't meaningless. These daily stories come from reporters talking to lots of people. Over time, a narrative, a story line emerges, which gives shape and meaning to all the contradictory information swirling in the market. The same holds for the economy. Beneath the swings in the business cycle, mood shifts in consumer confidence, and the billions and billions of price changes, there is an underlying, dominant price trend. This time it's deflation.

So, what is the deflation seismograph telling us? Deflation is built on three fundamental changes dating back to the late 1970s and early 1980s: (1) the embrace of market capitalism at home and abroad; (2) the spread of information technologies; and, most importantly for understanding the economy of the next half century, (3) the triumph of the financier. None of these factors is new, but what is surprising is how powerfully each change has informed and reinforced the other.

First is globalization—that abstruse, abstract word frequently invoked by everyone from politicians to business executives to trade protesters. Globalization is really the spread of market capitalism domestically and internationally. The "market revolution" in the United States dates back to the troubled, tumultuous decade of the 1970s, when double-digit inflation rates almost spiraled out of control, unemployment rose to its highest levels since the Great Depression, the economy stagnated and dropped into two severe recessions between 1973 and 1983, and the carefully constructed post–World War II international financial system fell apart. American companies stumbled horribly as industrial America, including the auto, steel, electronics, and machine tool industries, lost market share and profits to Japanese, German, and other overseas rivals. The sense grew that America had fallen into a long-term economic decline.

To attack stagnation, a growing number of economists, policy makers, and public scholars advocated unleashing the invisible hand of market forces and restraining the visible hand of government. Deregulation introduced competitive market pressures into formerly protected industries. In the 1970s, the U.S. government deregulated the energy and transportation industries; in the '80s and '90s, financial services and telecommunications.

Antitrust law was also relaxed. A hands-off government gave an opening to financial swashbucklers like T. Boone Pickens, Craig McCaw, Henry Kravis, Richard Rainwater, Ted Turner, Rupert Murdoch, and others to challenge an encrusted establishment in the 1980s. Junk bond king Michael Milken often financed the deals. The real power of the junk bond market and leveraged finance was the opportunity it gave ambitious risk takers to displace risk-averse managers. Indeed, the influence of the financial gunslingers extended far beyond their immediate deal making. For every successful leveraged buyout or harebrained hostile takeover, a dozen corporate chieftains got the message: Take risks or lose your job. In other words, restructure your workforce and start breaking down bureaucratic barriers; focus on core competencies and shed peripheral businesses; and work your capital smarter. The 1980s simultaneously marked the death rattle of an old industrial order and the emergence of a new entrepreneurial economy. The 1990s began with entrepreneurial upstarts like Meg Whitman of ebay and Jeff Bezos of Amazon.com, backed by venture capitalists like John Doerr, shaking up industry after industry by offering consumers a better deal.

The United States also expanded its commitment to open borders. Communism's collapse in Eastern Europe and the former Soviet Union, the embrace of freer markets by China's profit-loving mandarins, and the turn toward market capitalism by many authoritarian governments in the developing world led to enormous increases in global commerce, international investment, and immigration flows. For instance, in 1980, only 25% of developing countries were manufacturers. By 1998 that figure had swelled to 80%.[2] Trade as a percent of America's GDP—the sum of exports and imports of goods and services—was 13% in 1970. It is now around a third. America has absorbed more than one million immigrants a year for the past two decades. More than 12% of the American workforce was born overseas, and almost one in five residents speaks a language other than English at home. Immigrants supply both valuable high-tech and scientific talent from Silicon Valley to Route 128, as well as filling low-wage jobs in restaurants and hotels.

Taken altogether, competition for markets, profits, and jobs is white-hot, keeping managers and employees on their toes, encouraging creativity and pursuing efficiencies. Capitalist competition and innovation are a force for low everyday prices. The jargon phrase is that most companies lack "pricing power." A company that hikes prices without adding an innovative twist or creating a new need, loses customers to a more efficient rival. High-quality generic goods are taking sales away from high-priced brands. Online and offline entrepreneurs with a low-cost product or idea are squeezing margins in fragmented industries like travel. Steep prices on CDs, DVDs, and other high-tech products encourage technological piracy, reverse engineering, and file sharing, which eventually force industry giants to capitulate and take out the markdown pen. Global excess capacity for all manner of goods and services, old and new, is pulling prices down. "That excess capacity is a function of decades of development strategy by successful emerging economies, whereby they sought to create enough capacity to satisfy fully their own domestic needs plus a margin left over to serve exert markets," says James Griffin, consulting economist at ING Investment Management. "This goes beyond a low-frequency cycle; it is more like an era."[3]

It is this ratcheting up of capitalist competition that accounts for the rise of the second major factor behind deflation: the Internet and other advanced information technologies. The integrated circuit was invented in the late 1950s, IBM revolutionized computerized data processing with the development of the 360 series in the mid-1960s, and *Time* magazine named 1982 the "Year of the Computer" as personal computers gained widespread acceptance. Yet it wasn't until the 1990s, after a long gestation period and the commercial development of the Internet, that business finally started figuring out how to harness the power of high-tech gear by reorganizing the workplace. The Information Age came into being because intense price competition forced management to invest in high-tech gear to boost efficiency and shore up profits.

Innovation doesn't have a straight-line impact on growth. Picture this: a chart with an S-shaped curve. Whenever a major new technology is introduced into an economy or workplace, workers and managers struggle to master unfamiliar skills. Learning how to exploit a frontier technology takes years of experimentation and organizational reshuffling. Over time, though, both management and labor move up the experience curve. Gains in output per worker show up in lower prices and higher quality that in turn put additional downward pressure on prices. History offers striking examples of the S-curve effect. Take electricity. Many of the critical advances came in the 1880s. But it wasn't until years later that the productivity-enhancing promise of electrification was realized. Overall U.S. productivity jumped to a 2.4% annual rate in the early 1900s vs. a 1.3% pace in the late 1800s, according to Paul David, economic historian at Stanford University. "Society has to adapt around new technologies," says computer scientist Danny Hillis. "That takes longer than developing the technologies themselves."[4]

The high-tech sector actually lowers inflation as it becomes a bigger part of the economy. Falling prices are a way of life in the high-tech sector. For instance, in 2003 companies bought more than $300 billion in computers and peripherals measured at 1996 prices, calculates Brad DeLong, economist at the University of California, Berkeley. But these companies will actually fork out less than $100 billion in today's dollars for the high-tech gear. "Inflation would not be so very low today were it not for the falling prices of high-tech goods," writes DeLong. "These products make up such a large slice of the market's demand that their price trends matter."[5] Adds Mohan Sawhney, professor of technology at the Kellogg Graduate School of Management: "On the whole we are dealing with price deflation today. If you look at the aggregate numbers and the CPI, we're a couple of subpercentage points below zero for last year. Without the Internet, we would probably have been higher."

The third factor is a new international monetary system that washed out inflation. The new system is based on a shared commitment among central bankers that their job is to prevent inflation and keep prices stable. And the commitment needs to be firm and credible, since the link between currencies and a commodity like gold and silver was severed in the 1970s. Nations adopted a "fiat" system where the value of a dollar, mark, franc, yen, or other currency was backed by the full faith and credit of government.

Central bankers made a number of devastating mistakes in the early years of fiat money. But eventually central bankers in Washington and London, traders in New York and Shanghai, and investment bankers in Frankfurt and Chile came to share a common ideology or worldview: Inflation is always bad. In America, Paul Volcker and his successor, Alan Greenspan, gradually contained inflation through a long, cumulative process called disinflation, or lower inflation rates. The CPI for the major industrial nations peaked at more than 13% in 1980; by 2003, CPI inflation had declined to an average of less than 2%. The comparable figures for the United States were 14% and 1.5%, respectively. Business and consumer expectations of higher prices moderated over the years. Central bankers might disagree on technique, but all essentially decided that Milton Friedman was right when he said "inflation is everywhere and always a monetary phenomenon." They tapped into their control over money to fight price increases. "The Fed won't allow inflation," says Arthur Rolnick, head of research at the Federal Reserve Bank of Minneapolis. "If we had inflation going faster than 3%, we would have a heart attack. So would the world."

Rolnick's right. The commitment to price stability goes far beyond the abilities and desires of any central bank including the Fed. The monetary experts in academia, think tanks, and government are currently arguing fiercely whether to explicitly target an inflation rate of, say, 2% or allow for discretion by the monetary authorities. Canada and New Zealand publish their target inflation. America and Switzerland prefer to use policy discretion. Still, although there are some technical reasons why one or another monetary approach might be preferable, the difference doesn't matter all that much. Central banks have no choice but to contain inflation since the global capital markets are even more important than monetary policy in dampening inflationary pressures.

The fact is, investors abhor inflation since it degrades the value of their investment. So, in today's tightly integrated capital markets linked by satellite and fiber-optic communications networks that span the globe, financiers will flee any currency that shows signs of inflation. The global stock and bond markets are a giant voting machine that limits the ability of governments or central bankers to tolerate inflation. Investors force central bankers to stick with anti-inflation strategies. "Market actors are understandably sensitive to even the slightest sign of recidivism by governments," writes Benjamin J. Cohen, professor of international political economy at the University of California, Santa Barbara. "A commitment to 'sound' management, therefore, cannot easily be relaxed. States can never let down their guard if they are to establish and maintain a successful brand name for their money. In fact, a deflationary bias is regarded as an imperative of 'sound' management—simply the price to be paid for defending a currency's reputation."[6] James Carville, President Clinton's first campaign manager, made the same point, just more colorfully: "I used to think if there was reincarnation I wanted to come back as the President or the Pope or a .400 baseball hitter. But now I want to come back as the bond market. You can intimidate everyone."

The Payoff

The economic payoff partly came from the resurgence in productivity beginning in the 1990s, especially after 1995, which also marked the acceleration of the trend toward ever-lower inflation rates. Pro-

ductivity measures output per hour of work. It is the number economists really care about because the productivity growth rate is the
foundation of higher living standards. Strong productivity growth
translates over time into more output and lower prices. "Ultimately,
productivity growth is what determines our living standards, the
competitive advantage of companies, and the wealth of nations,"
says Erik Brynjolfsson, an economist at Massachusetts Institute of
Technology.[7]

The period 1948 to 1973 was a golden era of economic
growth. American productivity averaged close to 3% a year, a major
factor behind the 4% average annual growth rate in the economy.
Inflation was largely dormant until the Vietnam War in 1965 and
the OPEC oil shock of 1973. But productivity growth slumped
badly in the early 1970s. Wages stagnated, and any income gains
over the next two decades largely came from women entering the
workforce. Productivity eked out a 1.4% annual rate of growth from
1973 to 1995. "The standard of living by and large fell, stagnated, or
grew very slowly for most Americans, even though we were working
longer and harder," writes Jeffrey Madrick, author of *The End of
Affluence: The Causes and Consequences of America's Economic Decline*.[8]

Productivity revived during the new economy of the 1990s. For
instance, productivity ran at an average annual rate of 3% between
1995 and 2003. Now, the phrase "new economy" has fallen into disfavor after the bursting of the dot.com bubble. Many people believe it
was nothing but hype to spur stock sales and stock option pay packages. Yale University economist Robert Shiller scornfully dissected
"new era" proclamations in *Irrational Exuberance*, his exquisitely
timed warning against an overvalued stock market.[9] *New Yorker*
writer John Cassidy's bestseller *Dot.con*, a marvelous retelling of the
manic Internet boom and bust, dismissed the "new economy" enthusiasm of the past decade. "The New Economy arguments of the
1990s replicated those made during the 1920s, when they were
known as the 'new economics,' " wrote Cassidy.[10]

The problem with this jaundiced perspective is that the economy and Wall Street aren't the same. Sure, some dot.com stocks soared to absurd heights, and some commentators got carried away. But so what? Many good companies got funded, and they survived, and lots of business models and business ideas were tested in the market. Many former dot.comers distributed their Internet-related skills throughout the economy. Internet commerce has surpassed even the starry-eyed forecasts of the late 1990s. For instance, the widely derided 1999 prediction that e-commerce between businesses in the United States would reach a staggering $1.3 trillion in 2003 was $1 trillion too low by mid-2003.[11] Management moved up the learning curve, figuring out ways to tap into the economic benefits of information technologies. "Companies are really using the Internet," says Grady Means, chairman of MetaCap Partners. "They are networking. They are outsourcing. The net result? Prices don't go up." But productivity does.

What's more, experience and technology are even curing "Baumol's disease." William Baumol, a brilliant, soft-spoken economist who has spent his academic life at Princeton University and New York University, conceived an idea that explained poor service-sector productivity. Factories keep figuring out how to make more with less. The same can't be said for service businesses. Baumol's insight was to blame Mozart.[12] It still takes the same number of people and the same amount of time to play Mozart's *String Quartet in G Minor* as it did in 1787. Similarly, even as brewers bottled more beer with fewer workers, the number of consultants hired for a project didn't change all that much. Yet nurses, professors, insurance agents, classical musicians, and other service-sector workers in low-productivity professions have to be paid enough to prevent them from transferring their skills to more productive sectors of the economy.[13]

No more. Commercial service-sector productivity has soared in recent years. For one thing, measured by the size of the audience that can enjoy Mozart's *String Quartet in G Minor*, at most a few hundred could have listened to a Mozart concert in 1787. By the time the new economy came into full swing, the Emerson String Quartet could reach millions through the global technologies of radio, CDs, television, satellite hookups, and DVDs. More important, the vast sums of money invested in high-tech gear by financial services companies, business services, wholesale trade, insurance carriers, and other services are finally paying off, according to research by economists Jack E. Triplett and Barry P. Bosworth.[14] Innovations, including contracting out and outsourcing overseas, allow service companies to reduce costs, boost revenues, and improve their competitiveness. "We find that in post 1995 services industries labor productivity has proceeded at about the economy-wide rate," say Triplett and Bosworth. "Moreover, services industries have experienced an acceleration of labor productivity after 1995 that is comparable with the aggregate acceleration that has received so much attention."

To be sure, prices have been soaring in education and medical care services well in excess of the consumer price index. Productivity lags badly in both of these major service industries. But the sharp hike in tuition fees at major universities has partly been driven by the dire condition of state government coffers during 2000 to 2003. The pressure is easing as the economic expansion fills the government's tax till. Medical services inflation largely reflects a dysfunctional health care system, a badly frayed patchwork quilt of public, private, and nonprofit safety nets. Still, rising prices in these two vital sectors of the economy are nowhere near enough to offset the overall downward pressure on prices. Indeed, both the education and health industries are under enormous pressure to boost productivity, contain costs, and bring down prices.

The major beneficiary of the new economy is the consumer. Consumers have more choice, control, and information than before. The 21st century isn't the age of the industrialist, the financier, or even the entrepreneur. It's the age of the consumer. "Dramatic drop in production costs is nothing new: it happened before, say for automobiles and other industrial products," says Charles G. Goldfinger, founder of Global Electronic Finance, an international consulting firm. "What is new is that prices fall even more rapidly than costs. That means productivity gains are now largely captured by the consumer."[15]

You Ain't Seen Nothin' Yet

Conventional yardsticks underestimate prospects for prosperity during a deflationary era. For one thing, the American economy is at the early stages of a major technological revolution both in terms of actual technological innovations and, more important, in business, learning how to apply information technologies to boost their competitiveness.

Capital will be ample to fund entrepreneurial opportunities. After all, the share of the developed world's population in its high-savings years will increase with the aging of the baby boom generaion. An aging population is eager for high returns on their savings so that they can live well in retirement. Workers in the major industrial nations are also putting more and more of their savings into private pensions. America, the Netherlands, and Britain led the way in relying more on private pensions, but the trend is increasingly a European-wide phenomenon. Interest rates are likely to stay low, too. There was a saying in 19th-century Britain that "John Bull can stand many things, but he cannot stand 2%." British money eagerly sought out higher investment returns in emerging markets, such as America and Argentina. In a low interest rate environment investors will search for lush returns in higher-risk investments, such as in emerging markets like China and India.

Employment growth will be strong. And over the next two decades or so, demographics will favor anyone looking for a job. The baby boom generation is nearing retirement, and the cohort that follows is too small to fill employer demand. Now, boomers are increasingly looking at retirement as a transition to another work life, and not time spent on the golf course. Eight in ten baby boomers say they plan on working in retirement, according to the AARP, the giant lobbyist for the over-50 crowd. Nevertheless, business will constantly complain about labor shortages, much as they did during the latter part of the 1990s. For instance, the labor expert Anthony Carnevale, a vice president and researcher at Educational Testing Service, predicts a skilled worker gap of 5 million in 2010 and 14 million in 2020.[16]

The number of people trapped in poverty should shrink with fast growth. Thanks to a 4% growth rate and a 4% unemployment rate during the 1995 to 2000 boom, companies snapped up minorities, women, seniors, and anyone else willing to work for a day's pay. The once unemployable found jobs and the working poor showed a big rise in their wages. University of Texas political economist Paul Jargowsky calculates that the number of people living in high-poverty neighborhoods (with a poverty rate of 40% or higher) in the 1990s plunged by 24%, or 2.5 million people. The share of poor black individuals living in high-poverty neighborhoods dropped from 30% in 1990 to 19% in 2000.[17]

It's not just the U.S. economy that should do well. In the decades following the Bolshevik Revolution of 1917 and colonialism's end in the 1950s and 1960s, economic development efforts largely focused on central planning and government-led investment. And the best and brightest people from Brazil to the Soviet Union became government bureaucrats, military officers, lawyers, and members of other economically unproductive professions. When P. T. Bauer, the late development economist from the London School of Economics, lectured at a dozen or so Indian universities and research centers in 1970, teachers and students alike believed that central planning was indispensable for raising living standards—the only question was whether the Soviet or the Chinese model of development was superior.

Today, the balance of power has decisively shifted away from governments and toward markets. And when markets are large and laws allow people to easily build companies and keep their profits, more and more talented people become entrepreneurs, innovators, and wealth creators. On a global scale, freer trade will invigorate growth by providing entrepreneurs from all the world's major economies access to bigger markets. Trade also encourages the spread of new technologies and manufacturing techniques. The impact on growth could be staggering. Over the past two centuries, as national boundaries have shrunk in importance and open borders expanded, the pace of economic development has quickened. The United Kingdom needed nearly 60 years to double its output per person beginning in 1780. It took Japan 34 years starting in the 1880s, and South Korea only 11 years after 1966.

Take four nations where private enterprise is being unleashed: Brazil, Russia, India, and China. Each nation is trying to get the fundamentals right. Keep inflation low and fiscal policies prudent. Maintain high savings and investment rates. Improve the education level of the population. Trade with the outside world and encourage foreign direct investment. On the fast track for development, these four economies could be larger than the six largest industrial nations combined—the so-called G6—in less than 40 years. They are currently worth less than 15% of the G6 economies. Economists at the investment banking firm Goldman Sachs predict China will become the world's largest economy by 2041, assuming its growth rate slows from its pace of 8% or so to 5% in 2020 and 3.5% by the mid-2040s. India surpasses Japan in 2032. Of course, long-term projections are notoriously unreliable. Still, within several decades these countries could join the club of wealthy nations.[18]

The significance of a larger market, including the stock and bond markets, goes beyond trade and profit. With prices free of the distortion of inflation, the new environment is restoring prices to their traditional role as an economic arbiter: they are the signals that tell companies and individuals how the marketplace truly values the goods they make and the services they sell.

What's more, the financial market transforms experiments,

gossip, rumor, insight, tactics, strategies, information, and judgment into knowledge. The Austrian economist Friedrich Hayek emphasized the role the markets play in creating and disseminating knowledge. In the Information Age the cost of gathering and sharing information and knowledge has plummeted. "Capitalism, as Hayek conceived it, was fundamentally dynamic, and that dynamism was due to the discovery of new needs and new ways of fulfilling them by entrepreneurs possessed with 'resourcefulness,'" writes historian Jerry Muller.[19]

Indeed, knowledge and its application to real business problems count for more than capital and labor, the traditional factors of production. The more pervasive the markets the more information becomes easily available, and the better the market works at its fundamental task of transmitting valuable knowledge about everything from how to organize a productive factory to government policies that encourage growth to finding the life-transforming device being created in a garage in Shanghai, China. "Knowledge doesn't face diminishing returns. It's an expanding universe," says Richard Baldwin, economist at the Graduate Institute of International Studies in Geneva, Switzerland. Adds Paul Romer, economist at Stanford University and a leading theorist of growth: "We systematically underappreciate the potential for new things to happen."[20]

Of course, there will be plenty of missteps along the way during that process of discovery. The most spectacular explorations will be market bubbles reminiscent of the dot.com boom and bust. Bubbles are fascinating. The characteristic of any market bubble is well known: the rise in speculative fever; the piling into the hot investment of the moment to earn outsize rewards; and the crash, when prices plummet at a frightening speed. In hindsight, it's always puzzling how so many people could be so stupid with their money. How is it that investors during Web mania thought a price-earnings multiple of 100 was conservative, 1,000 plausible, and infinity conceivable? What transforms the normal propensity of "gamesters" to gamble into a gravity-defying speculative mania? The most common explanation is investor irrationality. The mass of investors simply take leave of their senses. In a now legendary phrase, with greed run amok, investors exhibit "irrational exuberance." As Gustave Le Bon put it in 1895, "In crowds, it is stupidity and not mother-wit that is accumulated."[21]

No doubt about it, enthusiasm spirals out of control during bubbles. But maybe investors aren't quite as stupid as their critics maintain. "Do we really believe that the New York Stock Exchange and the NASDAQ are temples to irrationality?" asks John H. Cochrane, finance professor at the University of Chicago.[22] Speculations often emerge during times of major innovations and technological progress. The price gains are largely driven by the economic fundamentals and not investor irrationality. British economist John Maynard Keynes once cautioned not to fret excessively about speculative zeal when the underlying economy is strong. "Speculators may do no harm as bubbles are on a steady stream of enterprise. But the position is serious when enterprise becomes the bubble on a whirlpool of speculation."[23]

Take Tulipmania. The Dutch rush to invest in rare tulip bulbs in the mid-1630s is perhaps the most remarkable story in the history of finance. Charles Mackay's 1841 classic, *Extraordinary Popular Delusions and the Madness of Crowds,* memorably describes the tulip bulb speculation. "Every one imagined that the passion for tulips would last for ever," he wrote. "Nobles, citizens, farmers, mechanics, seamen, footmen, maid-servants, even chimney sweeps and old clotheswomen, dabbled in tulips."[24] Tulip bulb prices soared into the stratosphere. The speculative frenzy suddenly ended in February 1637, and prices tumbled sharply lower as speculators panicked. "The collapse of tulip prices had a chilling effect on Dutch economic life in the years that followed—there ensued, in modern terminology, an appreciable depression," writes economist John Kenneth Galbraith in *A Short History of Financial Euphoria.*[25]

The problem is, much of Mackay's history reflects literary license. Economic historians also agree that the price swings had almost no impact on the Dutch economy. Holland dominated the new market for tulips, and the high prices were for particularly beautiful and rare varieties that came from the mosaic virus (an infection poorly understood at the time). Speculative trading activity in rare bulbs surged along with strong demand, much of it coming from French fashion. Prices declined sharply after rapid reproduction or the introduction of new varieties. For instance, some rare tulip bulb prices in 1707 converged toward the prices of valuable bulbs at the market peak of 1637, only to decline at a rapid rate over the next 15 years. The same price phenomenon is at work in many markets today, from prize bulls to thoroughbred horses to flowers. In 1987 a small quantity of prototype lily bulbs were sold in Holland for $693,000 (in 1999 prices)—the cost of a McMansion in a tony suburb. To be sure, there was a one-month spectacular surge and sudden decline in common tulip bulb prices toward the end of Tulipmania that can't be explained by the economic fundamentals, says Peter Garber, author of *Famous First Bubbles*. He adds that any fallout from the precipitous price decline was contained because the courts did not uphold informal futures contracts for tulips.

Economic historians still debate just what went on in the Mississippi Bubble and the South Sea Bubble of the early 1700s. Both are complicated tales full of power and intrigue. The schemes involved refinancing war debt from governments essentially bankrupt from waging war, the French government with the Mississippi Bubble and the British government with the South Sea Bubble. In each case, a company expanded rapidly through corporate takeovers and the acquisition of government debt. Selling successive waves of stock to an eager public financed the expansion. Both eventually collapsed from too much leverage and too little opportunity. Yet were these projects truly bubbles? John Law, perhaps the world's first Keynesian, was the architect of the Mississippi Bubble and his ideas informed the South Sea Bubble. In a capital-scarce world, Law believed, finance came first, and that the expansion of circulating credit was a primary force behind economic growth. His idea remains a centerpiece of most modern economic textbooks, and plans to modernize an economy through financial innovation and fiscal reform are commonplace—just ask the International Monetary Fund. Powerful government officials also backed each venture. Yes, the financing eventually unraveled and the promised commercial returns didn't materialize. But that's far from saying investors took leave of their senses.

Similarly, much of the scorn directed toward irrational exuberance in the 1990s misses the point. Sure, we can all exchange stories about crazy investors and absurd valuations. The three-year-long bear market was extraordinarily painful. Yet with the benefit of hindsight, it's clear that the U.S. stock market's lofty valuations in the 1990s were anchored to the fundamentals of higher productivity and a long economic expansion. The bubble moralizers greatly underestimate the vital role of speculative markets in allocating resources toward an economy's fast-growing sectors and away from stagnant industries. Indeed, the current enthusiasm of Corporate America to invest in China has all the earmarks of a bubble. American companies are pouring resources into China, outsourcing production for global markets and establishing a local presence to sell goods and services to its 1.3 billion people. China is the place to be (along with India), and a lucrative consulting industry has sprung up to encourage American managers to invest billions and billions into the Asian giant. But China faces enormous economic challenges, including bad bank loans as high as 40% of GDP, the prospect of mass unemployment as rural residents migrate to the cities, and pressure to revalue its currency.[26] Many investments by American headquartered companies won't pay off or will go sour. Yet the enthusiasm for China is accelerating the construction of strong economic ties between the two giant markets, bridges that will strengthen in coming decades. Along the way, fortunes will be made and lost. Investments will coin money or vanish. But what's going on is real. There is a steady stream of enterprise underlying the surge in investment into China.

The Economic Mindset

How fast can the economy grow without generating inflation? How low can unemployment go? No one really knows. But the odds are that the economy can grow faster than most economists think, and unemployment can go lower than traditional models predict. Much of mainstream economics falls short in dealing with the impact of the kind of momentous upheaval I'm describing. The kinds of models that predict a set limit to noninflationary growth describe a world where the economy plods ahead at a rate determined by the amount of capital and labor employed, while fiscal and monetary policies are geared toward keeping the economy's fluctuations within a fairly narrow band.

Of course, conventional models do an excellent job of describing how interest rates affect home buying or how higher taxes crimp consumer spending. Yet the language of economics is full of metaphors and constructs that suggest too much growth is a bad thing, such as the economy's speed limit (how fast the economy can grow before inflation takes off), the noninflationary rate of employment growth (how low unemployment can go before inflation surges higher), or its growth potential (inflation will surge if an economic growth exceeds its potential).[27] And many of the answers were established when inflation was the primary price trend.

Take the notion that too many people holding down a job and producing more goods and services debauches the currency and reduces the purchasing power of money. The belief that there's an inevitable trade-off between economic growth and inflation largely rests on the theoretical foundation of NAIRU, or the nonaccelerating inflation rate of unemployment. The NAIRU idea took deep root when inflation soared into double-digit territory in the 1970s. Here's the basic idea: In any economy, worker preferences, job changes, labor market institutions, and other factors add up to a "natural" rate of unemployment. The natural rate is defined as the jobless rate consistent with stable prices. When the unemployment rate drops below its natural rate, wage pressures build and inflation takes off. You can almost hear Karl Marx muttering, "I told you so! Capitalism needs a 'reserve army of the unemployed.' "

So where is the "natural rate" of unemployment? A few years ago, many mainstream economists assumed it was somewhere between 6% and 6.5%. But unemployment fell below 4% even as the inflation rate fell in the late 1990s. Economist Robert Eisner called NAIRU "the greatest misconception of all." Eisner suggested that the unemployment–inflation relationship is asymmetric. High unemployment is associated with lower inflation rates. But low unemployment doesn't tell us much—if anything—about the future direction of inflation. "Can I guarantee that measures—short of war—to reduce unemployment to 3.4% will not increase the rate of inflation? No!" said Eisner. "Can anyone be sure it will increase inflation, let alone by how much, or that the inflation will continue accelerating? I daresay no."[28]

Simply put, economic growth does not cause inflation. The odds are that many concepts developed when inflation was a major problem will become footnotes during a deflationary era. The historic record suggests that deflation and economic growth can go hand in hand. But as we will see, the coming deflation is far from nirvana. For one thing, the inevitable downturn in a capitalist economy could be brutal as prices plummet. Even more important, the deflationary world that is evolving is an insecure one. Rapid economic growth and worker insecurity are two sides of the same coin during deflation.

CHAPTER 5

THE RISE IN INSECURITY

It was the best of times, it was the worst of
times, it was the age of wisdom, it was the age
of foolishness, it was the epoch of belief, it
was the epoch of incredulity, it was the season
of Light, it was the season of Darkness, it
was the spring of hope, it was the winter of
despair, we had every-thing before us, we had
nothing before us, we were all going direct
to Heaven, we were all going direct the
other way.

—CHARLES DICKENS

MY MEMORY OF WHERE I WAS IS HAZY. BUT ON
one of my many business trips, I ended up on the
set of a local public radio call-in show. The host
was personable and the topic was the outlook for
the economy as well as personal finance. I think
it was the first caller who asked, "Okay, can you
explain to me what are we supposed to do to get the economy growing: save more or spend more? We're lectured about not saving
enough, but then we're also told to buy more. So which is it?" My
answer, for what it is worth, is that much of the save more versus
spend more discussion is beside the point. I recalled an economics
seminar I had attended several years ago when Joseph Stiglitz, later

to become a Nobel laureate, went through the six different iterations that the administration of President Bush (the elder) had used to justify a cut in the capital gains tax rate over the years, beginning with boosting savings and ending with increasing spending.

What does matter? Creativity. Innovation. Competitiveness. The discovery of new ways of organizing business. Finding new wants to meet. That's where economic growth comes from, not from ticks up or down in savings or spending.

The most famous proponent of this way of looking at economic life is Joseph Schumpeter, one of the 20th century's intellectual giants. He believed that innovation and risk taking were the essence of capitalism. Schumpeter has become a leading light to a group of growth theorists: economists such as Paul Romer of Stanford, Gene Grossman of Princeton, and Richard Nelson of Columbia. Schumpeter is best known for his evocative metaphor "creative destruction." It captures the process by which new technologies, new markets, and new organizations supplant the old. Many economists and Wall Street financiers rightly celebrated the gains from creative destruction during the 1990s, with a heavy emphasis on creative. After all, who doesn't like creativity?

The Dark Side of Creativity

Less appreciated is that Schumpeter also emphasized the destruction side of the equation. The dynamism of capitalist competition is devastatingly painful. While 17th-century textile makers in Britain built the factory system, middle-class weavers in Yorkshire sank into poverty. In the 1800s, the spread of railroads devastated communities without a rail link. The 1950s and 1960s were an era of U.S. economic dominance, but many industrial laborers never recovered from losing the well-paying manufacturing jobs held by thousands of them before industrial companies moved from the Northeast and

Midwest to cheaper sites in the South and West. Today, highly educated 24/7 technology workers are losing jobs to lower-paid 24/7 peers in the developing world. "It is hard to think of a technological advance that did not reduce the value of someone's specific assets and skills," writes economic historian Joel Mokyr.[1]

Deflation is a stern taskmaster that increases both the rewards to creativity and the risk of destruction. Earlier, we saw how deflationary capitalism flourished in the United States and the European core countries in the 19th century. Revolutions in agriculture, industry, science, and commerce created immense wealth and raised overall living standards. But not everyone benefited. Far from it. Living conditions plunged for many farmers who lost their land as falling commodity prices wiped them out. Rural residents flocked to cities looking for work and settled into dangerous, disease-infested slums. Jacob Riis described New York City's slums in 1890 in *How the Other Half Lives.*[2]

> If it shall appear that the sufferings and the sins of the "other half," and the evil they breed, are but as a just punishment upon the community that gave it no other choice, it will be because that is the truth. The boundary line lies there because, while the forces for good on one side vastly outweigh the bad—it were not well otherwise—in the tenements all the influences make for evil; because they are the hot-beds of the epidemics that carry death to rich and poor alike; the nurseries of pauperism and crime that fill our jails and police courts; that throw off a scum of forty thousand human wrecks to the island asylums and workhouses year by year; that turned out in the last eight years a round half million beggars to prey upon our charities; that maintain a standing army of ten thousand tramps with all that that implies; because, above all, they touch the family life with deadly moral contagion.

Men, women, and children labored long, hard hours in dank factories. Unscrupulous financiers squandered the savings of millions in unsavory manipulations. Economic downturns, called "panics" back then, were brutal with no government safety net. Large corporations wielded immense political power. Income inequality widened precipitously. The substantial progress achieved through raw Darwinian capitalism carried a steep human price in misery, lives cut short, and dreams dashed. The turmoil and hardship spawned a variety of powerful protest movements and radical political parties, especially Marxism and socialism in Europe and populism and progressivism in the United States.

America experienced a number of downturns between 1873 and 1897, as well as several financial panics, including a famous episode in 1907. Like post–World War II recessions, no two downturns were exactly alike. Yet there were some striking commonalities. Economic upturns were associated with investment booms funding major innovations such as the capital-intensive railroads. Intrepid innovators and swashbuckling entrepreneurs made enormous profits, promoters and swindlers took advantage of growing enthusiasm with various financial schemes, and the investment frenzy swelled—until reality set in. In the United States, with thousands of state and national banks and no central bank, downturns usually led to widespread bank failures. Hundreds of banks would go out of business as their assets plunged in value and nervous depositors lined up to take their money out. The overall price level typically plunged, sometimes precipitously.[3]

The average person became increasingly vulnerable to economic downturns as the 19th century progressed. By the 1890s, America had made the transition from an agricultural economy to an industrial one. Many aspects of life were improving. Wages were up by a healthy 25% to 28% from 1890 to 1900 (taking into account both wage hikes and the decrease in living costs). But the downside risk from losing a job or taking a pay cut also went up significantly. Fewer families were self-sufficient and more households relied on a steady paycheck earned in a factory or on a construction crew to make ends meet. Thus, getting fired hit hard. "These particularly bad times not only saw monumental strikes, but also demonstrations in American cities by the unemployed—who represented upwards of 30 percent of the workforce—for public relief programs and work projects," says historian Walter Licht.[4]

Strikes were frequent as conflicts broke out between management and labor. The most violent took place in the last deflationary quarter of the century. Businesses and their political allies didn't hesitate to call out the militia or federal troops to break strikes. For instance, the great railroad strike of 1877 started in Martinsburg, West Virginia, when workers protested a 10% wage cut imposed in concert by managers of the major rail companies. The strike spread like wildfire, jumping to Buffalo, Pittsburgh, Chicago, St. Louis, Galveston, San Francisco, and other cities across the country. In just two weeks the strike claimed at least 50 lives, saw hundreds injured, and landed thousands in jail. The most famous bloody strike of the time took place at Andrew Carnegie's modern steel plant, Homestead Works. The price of steel had dropped by 37% between 1890 and 1892. Carnegie and his right-hand man, Henry Frick, wanted to cut costs by breaking the Amalgamated Association of Iron and Steel. Frick locked out the employees in 1892; the union took over the mill; the workers won a pitched fight against a private army of Pinkerton security employees; but the strike was over when the state militia seized the plant and strikebreakers took over.

Life was also hard on the farm. Agricultural prices fell sharply. Wheat came down from a dollar in the early 1870s to 70 cents in the late 1880s. Corn went from around 70 cents a bushel in the early 1870s down to 30 cents in the 1890s. Many farms failed, and agricultural protest movements swept the frontier. The anger was directed at railroads, banks, grain operators, commodities brokers, land speculators, and the Eastern Establishment's gold standard. An excerpt from the 1882 "Anti-Monopoly War Song" captures the farmer's dismay and protest.[5]

Farmers, ye who sow the plain
With its wealth of precious grain,
Yet must see your fruit of toil
Be the Rail-Roads' robber-spoil,
Onward! onward to the fray!
Hurl the monster from your way,
Let your cry of battle be
Ruin to monopoly!

The discontent profoundly shaped the political environment. Still, economic historians now believe the popular perception of widespread disaster among farmers is exaggerated. Agricultural prices did fall, but so did costs. The value of farmland rose by 75% between 1870 and 1890, and by another 25% over the next decade. The evidence on railroads is mixed, but freight costs came down as a percent of farm prices. Farmers in the West did pay higher rates on their mortgages than in the East, but the differential partly reflected higher risk, not predatory lending. Real incomes in agriculture rose, albeit at a slow pace.[6]

None of this is to say that farmers weren't aggrieved. They were living in a time of creative destruction. Farming was increasingly mechanized. The cost of taking on the debt to buy high-tech gear strained cash flow. The farmer was also tightly tied to the national and global markets in the late 19th century. Intensely competitive impersonal global market forces now determined farm sales and farm prices, heightening a sense that farmers no longer controlled their destiny, no matter how hard they worked the fields. A bumper crop in Prussia or Russia could hammer crop prices at home. The level of uncertainty in an intrinsically uncertain business went up. So did the desire for government to alleviate the uncertainty.

No wonder a populist revolt spread among farmers, workers, and small business. The progressive movement—a loose coalition of farmers, organized labor, urban lower classes, and a segment of the middle-class business community—worked to strengthen government power to offset the power of big business and Wall Street financiers. Farmers and laborers blamed many of their troubles on deflation—falling prices, declining wages, and job losses. The rallying cry became bring on inflation by changing the monetary system—that's right, money policy dominated American politics in the late 19th century—from the classic gold standard to a gold and silver standard. Populists argued that a bimetal standard would increase the supply of money and therefore cause higher prices. Inflation was the economic panacea that would solve many problems. Inflation, they argued, would ease the burden of debt and raise incomes. The silver plan was bitterly opposed by the industrialists, financiers, and East Coast establishment, since inflation would depreciate the value of their investments. Many Americans also seemed to instinctively recoil from any monetary scheme designed to create inflation, scarred by memories of the ruinous inflations of the Revolutionary War and the Civil War, as well as hyperinflation in the waning days of the Confederacy.

The high moment of the free silver movement came when Democratic presidential candidate William Jennings Bryan, a powerful speaker, transfixed the Democratic National Convention with his legendary "Cross of Gold" speech in 1896: "Having behind us the producing masses of this nation and the world, supported by the commercial interests, the laboring interests and the toilers everywhere, we will answer their demand for a gold standard by saying to them: You shall not press down upon the brow of labor this crown of thorns, you shall not crucify mankind upon a cross of gold."[7]

Deflation was so common that one of America's favorite children's stories is shot through with allegorical references to deflation and inflation. *The Wizard of Oz* was written by former South Dakota newspaperman L. Frank Baum and first published in 1900. A number of scholars, including Henry Littlefield, Gretchen Ritter, and Hugh Rockoff, persuasively argue that the book is an allegory of monetary politics in the 1890s. Dorothy is the common person.

The scarecrow is the average farmer. The tin man is an industrial worker. The cowardly lion is William Jennings Bryan, the loquacious and ineffective politician. The cyclone that rips Dorothy's drab Kansas house from the prairie to Oz represents depression-era foreclosures. The wizard is President McKinley. Oz is the measure of gold and silver, the ounce. The MGM movie changed a key detail from the book: In the book Dorothy wore silver slippers, not ruby red. Thus, when she set out on the golden road to Oz, she and her friends were mixing silver and gold. But Baum, while sympathetic to the plight of farmers and workers, wasn't a diehard silver-or-bust populist. Dorothy loses her silver slippers on the way back home. The monetary solution of silver was no longer needed since the discovery of gold in Alaska eased price pressures and the economy revived.[8]

Bryan ran on the Democratic ticket against William McKinley, the Republican candidate and a supporter of the gold standard. Bryan lost badly. The silver movement died, but the populist and progressive reforms championed by Bryan and others gradually changed the economy and society. The political and social agitation eventually led to creation of an income tax system, the founding of a central bank, the passage of the Sherman Anti-Trust Act, and the eight-hour work day. The spread of high school education and enormous investments in college and universities also stem from this period. In 1910 fewer than 10% of young people graduated from high school. Yet by 1940 the median 18-year-old in America was a high school graduate.[9]

Why were protests so bitter and widespread in the latter part of the 19th century? There were many reasons, but the basic problem was income insecurity. There was a lot of creative destruction going on because of the "frenetic pace of technological change," says historian Robert Fogel. A lot of workers and farmers had a stake in existing ways of doing business. Jobs were lost to new technologies. Consider this 1829 letter from Martin Van Buren, governor of New York, to President Andrew Jackson.[10]

To: President Jackson

The canal system of this country is being threatened by the spread of a new form of transportation known as "railroads." The federal government must preserve the canals for the following reasons:

ONE If canal boats are supplanted by "railroads," serious unemployment will result. Captains, cooks, drivers, hostlers, repairmen and lock tenders will be left without means of livelihood, not to mention the numerous now employed in growing hay for horses.

TWO Boat builders would suffer and towline, whip and harness makers would be left destitute.

THREE Canal boats are absolutely essential to the defense of the United States. In the event of expected trouble with England, the Erie Canal would be the only means by which we could ever move the supplies so vital to waging modern war.

As you may well know, Mr. President, "railroad" carriages are pulled at the enormous speed of 15 miles per hour by "engines" which, in addition to endangering life and limb of passengers, roar and snort their way through the countryside, setting fire to crops, scaring the livestock and frightening women and children. The Almighty certainly never intended that people should travel at such breakneck speed.

Martin Van Buren, Governor of New York

Major new technologies create new wealth as they take their place in the economy, but not without displacing the skills and business of workers and companies. The Bessemer furnace is a famous example. For much of the 19th century, the railroads relied on cast iron, a brittle material that easily cracked. Steel was too expensive for mass production until the Bessemer method came along. The technologically advanced and economical Bessemer system replaced wrought iron, especially in the last part of the 19th century. Progress came with a steep price tag, however, notes economic historian Robert Fogel.

> While the Bessemer furnace increased the demand for workers at steel mills, it led to the loss of jobs in iron mills and foundries that could not compete with new steel products. The same kind of turmoil was created in petroleum, meatpacking, textiles, transportation vehicles, and wholesale and retail distribution. Moreover, numerous handicraft skills were made obsolete by the development of machines that could perform the same functions more quickly and more cheaply. Although far more new jobs were created than old jobs lost, those who obtained new jobs were often new immigrants, and those who lost the old jobs were often either native-born workers or longtime residents.[11]

It took the Great Depression for government to step in to help shelter workers from economic catastrophe. The Great Depression is the fault line in American economic history. Economist John Kenneth Galbraith wasn't exaggerating when he nominated the Great Depression as "the most important event in the century so far."[12] The qualifier "so far" is no longer needed now that we're in the next millennium.

The modern mixed economy came out of the Great Depression. A series of reforms that started with President Franklin D. Roosevelt's New Deal have prevented the inevitable downturns in a capitalist economy from turning into another devastating depression. America has had 10 recessions in the post–World War II era, with the deepest slump being a decline of 3% of gross domestic product in 1973–75 compared to nearly a drop of a third between 1929 and 1933. Among the most important reforms were the rise of the social safety net including unemployment insurance and Social Security; financial restructurings such as federal deposit insurance and the strengthening of the Federal Reserve system; and a federal government committed to combating downturns by running a budget deficit by cutting taxes or increasing spending, or both. The huge increase in the public sector provided a buffer or cushion that didn't previously exist against the inevitable downward swings in the business cycle. Workers enjoyed an unprecedented level of security in the early post–World War II decades.

The Great Depression also invigorated economics. Yes, everyone loves to make fun of the practitioners of the "dismal science." President Harry Truman famously quipped, "I want a one-armed economist so that the guy could never make a statement and then say 'on the other hand.' " Book publisher Alfred A. Knopf remarked that an "economist is a man who states the obvious in terms of the incomprehensible." Then there's the saying I hear all the time: "If all economists were laid end to end, they would not reach a conclusion."

Yet in the post–World War II era, economists became key advisors to governments. Economists are critical in international institutions such as the International Monetary Fund and the World Bank. The Federal Reserve is the largest employer of economists in the United States. Ivory tower economists such as Paul Samuelson, Franco Modigliani, and William Sharpe transformed our understanding of Wall Street, and their insights led to such revolutions as modern portfolio theory and the financial derivatives revolution. Modern macroeconomics, the study of economic growth, the rise and decline of economies, the direction of employment, prices, and output, came out of the Great Depression. John Maynard Keynes, Milton Friedman, James Tobin, Simon Kuznets, and George Stigler, to name only a few leading lights, successfully wrestled with how best to prevent a recurrence of that cataclysmic economic disaster.

As we've seen, the U.S. economy shares some intriguing parallels with the fast-growing deflationary economy of the 19th century. Growth prospects in the 21st century are probably even better than in the late 19th century. The acceleration of productivity since 1995 suggests that the economy can grow at a heady pace without generating inflation for years to come.

Yet, much like the 19th century, a souped-up economy translates into intense job insecurity from the warehouse floor to the white-collar office. Restructuring, downsizing, reengineering—whatever term you prefer—is now a routine part of management's strategic and tactical tool kit. Management is increasingly comfortable with allocating money and employment to profitable divisions and slashing investment and jobs in lagging sections of the company. Companies are vulnerable to a new technology rendering their traditional business obsolete. The pressure on management is relentless. A social safety net designed for a time when competition was limited, jobs secure, corporate loyalty a reality, and the husband worked while the wife stayed at home no longer works in the new economy.

The competition is heating up for producing the kind of high-quality goods and sophisticated services that the industrial nations have traditionally dominated. Cities such as Singapore, Penang in Malaysia, and Taipei in Taiwan are hotbeds of engineering talent. Many tech-savvy, well-compensated workers in America are fast becoming an expensive anachronism as tomorrow's technological advance offers new opportunities for slashing costs and improving economies of scale. A world filled with smart computers, all linked via the Internet, could easily undermine whole sectors of the service and information industries. "The types of risks that used to be confined to the blue-collar workforce are beginning to spread their tentacles into the necktie class," says Brad DeLong, an economist at the University of California at Berkeley.

When I wrote a column for *Business Week* in 2003 arguing against blaming foreign competition for the loss of jobs in 2003 and proposing a greater government investment in education and training, the reaction was immediate and vehement.[13]

You're looking at the problem through the eyes of an economist who probably never leaves his office or city to see the problems globalism is creating here in the States. I would rather pay $5 more for that T-shirt made here in America and have a well-paid job than be unemployed or make less and buy a T-shirt made in China for $3. I hope this example isn't too complicated for you to understand the dire situation we're facing here in the job market.

I have a bachelor's degree in computer science as well as an MBA. I'm SICK of going to school and I don't need NEW training. Because I chose to become a programmer, I have no hope of holding a job for the long run. I absolutely love my job (I'm in the 30% camp that does) and I do not relish the idea of losing this one, even if the "creative destruction" might get me something better (after losing my house, cars, and family from unemployment while someone in India lives like a king with my old job).

At some point, the "outflow" of jobs becomes a flood, and—to carry the water analogy a step further—we are left high and dry, overpriced in labor, materials, and finished products, no one to sell to, and too few people with jobs and paychecks to buy anything. . . . I'm one of those people who can see my job going to India in a year or two; I can even tell you the name and phone number of the person who will probably get my job.

The jobs of the future will be high tech and high skilled—but no matter how highly competent an American kid becomes, there will be someone in India or China who can do the job for a tenth of the cost. No job other than "hands on" can compete with low wages, so

exactly what jobs will remain, even if kids get educated?
It does not seem possible unless Americans work for
drastically reduced wages because creative destruction is
not a locally geographic occurrence, but a global one, and
"bottom line" economics means lowest wage wins.

Of course, there have been many other job scares that didn't pan
out. Automation in the 1950s and 1960s was supposed to lead to
massive unemployment. So was "unfair" competition from the Japanese competitors in the 1980s. The history of the U.S. economy suggests jobs will be created a lot faster than they are destroyed. Going
offshore is another organizational innovation taking advantage of
information technologies. A study by Diana Farrell of McKinsey
concludes that at least two-thirds of the economic benefit from outsourcing will flow back to the United States in terms of lower costs
and prices, new export opportunities, repatriated earnings, and new
jobs in the country.[14]

All this is cold comfort to anyone who loses a job to a machine,
a neighboring state, or an overseas worker. And when laid-off workers do find new jobs, these positions are often at a fraction of their
previous wage. The Bureau of Labor Statistics estimates that of
workers who were displaced by trade from 1979 to 1999, a little
more than half were at best working for 85% of their former wage.

The insecurity doesn't just stem from spells of unemployment
or reduced wages. America's health care system for working-age
families is employer based. So, when workers lose their jobs, they
also lose their health care coverage. When workers lose their jobs,
they join the more than 40 million Americans without health insurance. And those who keep their jobs are paying a soaring premium
price tag for coverage. An employer-based health insurance system
is both inefficient and inequitable. Once they are laid off, workers
can also no longer participate in their 401(k), 403(b), or comparable
retirement savings plan at work.

Another factor adding to the pall of worry is "money illusion."

The key to understanding money illusion is the difference between "real" prices and "nominal" prices. Let's use the example of wages. The nominal wage is your paycheck. The real wage is your paycheck adjusted for inflation. So, if you are used to a wage increase of 3% and all of a sudden your employer only grants wage hikes of 1%, you feel bad. But if inflation was running at 3% when you got a 3% raise, you got no raise at all. And if deflation was running at 1% and you got a 1% wage hike, you really got a 2% increase. Indeed, one factor behind late 19th–century labor strife was that people did not appreciate that difference. Yes, the "nominal" wage was falling, but the "real" wage was rising.

Money illusion can be a problem during major transitions from one economy to another, although I'm skeptical about its staying power. It's usually wrong to underestimate the financial savvy of workers and consumers over time. A far more useful concept than money illusion might be the "rule-of-thumb" perspective put forward by the late Fisher Black, a financial economist. With time, through conversation, reading, and experience, people evolve relatively sophisticated rules of thumb that capture the essence of what is going on in the money economy. "Because there is so much noise in the world, people adopt rules of thumb. They share their rules of thumb with each other, and very few people have enough experience with interpreting noisy eveidence to see that the rules are too simple. Over time, I expect that transmission through the media and through the schools of scientific ways of interpreting evidence will gradually make the rules of thumb more sophisticated," said Black.[15]

Central Bank Nervousness

Central bankers are also worried about a deflationary economy. One reason is that deflation redistributes income from debtors to creditors. Debt becomes increasingly expensive to pay back because of the critical difference between nominal interest rates and real interest rates. Nominal interest rates are what you read in the newspaper or what a bank will charge you for taking out a loan. So, if you took advantage of the 0%, 1.9%, or 2.9% financing available on many cars in recent years, that is your nominal interest rate. The same goes with credit-card rates at 9%, 13%, and 20%.

Economists believe the interest rate that truly matters is the "real" interest rate or the interest rate after subtracting inflation. That is what it really costs borrowers to pay back their loans. So, if you're paying a 10% nominal interest rate but inflation is rising at a 5% pace, the real rate of interest is 5%. If your nominal rate is at 5% and inflation is at 6%, the real rate of interest is negative. By the way, real rates did go negative during the 1970s, which is when it became conventional wisdom to borrow as much as possible, say to buy a bigger house than you needed. The rule of thumb was right, too, for despite the high interest rates of that era, the real cost of paying back debt shrank over time.

But what if nominal rates are at 2% and deflation is at 2%? The real rate is 4%. In effect, the real rate can rise above the market rate during deflations. The cost of paying back borrowed dollars becomes more expensive and more onerous. The greater the deflation, the higher the real interest rate, the more difficult it is for borrowers to service their debts, and the greater the risk of a bankruptcy epidemic. Similarly, the real cost to a company of paying a worker's wage goes up even if nominal wages stay the same. Since most workers are reluctant to accept a lower nominal wage, a higher "real" wage forces companies to lay off workers in an attempt to shore up profit margins.

Here's the potential dynamic of falling prices that gives central bankers nightmares: The danger is that consumers will hold off making purchases, at first convinced that prices will be lower next month or next year, and later because they're worried about losing their jobs; demand for goods and services falters, profits disappear, and companies start slashing investment plans and jobs; heavily indebted businesses and consumers fall behind on their payments; bank credit dries up as the default rate mounts; spending plans and wages are cut; prices drop some more; and so on, in a lethal economic downturn. A Federal Reserve memo during the 1937 downturn captured the basic dynamic well: "Plants are closing every day. Thousands of industrial workers are being laid off every day. Forward orders are being cancelled. . . . Prices are falling. . . . Such movements gather their own momentum, and feed on themselves."[16]

The real rate of interest stood for a time at 10% or more in the 1930s. The real value of household liabilities between 1929 and 1930—mortgages, consumer credit, and the like—soared by 20%. Little wonder defaults and debt delinquencies were commonplace among business, homeowners, farmers, and state and local governments. Almost every bank in the country was either shuttered or operated under tightly restricted conditions.

A reading of deflation history suggests that deflation is most dangerous when it is unexpected. If business, consumers, investors, and borrowers can plan for deflation, the disruption to business plans and economic activity could be minimal. The same holds if deflation is mild. The same can't be said for a surprise, which was the case in the Great Depression. Hardly anyone expected the economy to fall off a cliff or deflation to get as bad as it did.

For example, after reading the business press following the stock market crash, historian Daniel Nelson concludes that most people expected a mild deflation up until the mid-1930s.[17] A study by economists Adam Klug, John S. Langdon-Lane, and Eugene N. White into survey data on railroad freight car shipment forecasts found that industry missed the depression. The railroad business, the nation's largest at the time, was the most sophisticated industry in the world.

> It appears that business continued to expect the economy to begin a recovery and that the shift in the level of activity took a long time to accept. The magnitude of

the collapse appears to have been beyond the public comprehension, as all recoveries within recent experience had begun after a few quarters. Like professional forecasters and investors in futures markets, railroad managers failed to forecast the depression, expecting it to follow the pattern of recent recessions.[18]

Right now, one concern about deflation is that it would be unexpected and America is a highly indebted society. The value of household and nonfinancial corporate debt climbed to almost 180% of GDP in 2003. A half century ago, debt was 60% of GDP. Now, a lot of people love to criticize Americans for taking on too much debt. But it often makes sense. For instance, the recent housing boom was driven by low mortgage rates, which were almost as low as they were in the 1950s. Fierce competition in the home mortgage market has lowered fees and loosened down-payment requirements. Many households cashed in hefty equity gains, selling existing homes to trade up to better dwellings. Consumer and mortgage interest and principal payments absorbed about 14% of disposable income in the early 2000s, which is measurably higher than the 12% of the mid-1990s. Still, the move was rational, considering the price history of housing, low mortgage interest rates, and consumer incomes. But if hyperdeflation emerged, meeting those debt payments would turn onerous.

Another concern is that monetary policy is less effective at fighting deflation than inflation. Monetary policy is complex, with its own arcane language and opaque finances, and the impact of changes in monetary policy only work over time and through indirect ways. Economists still argue over the concept of money itself, let alone how to measure it. But the basic idea—and problem during a deflation—is fairly simple. The modern-day Fed largely runs monetary policy by setting a target rate for the federal funds rate, which is the interest rate that banks pay each other for borrowing money overnight. If the Fed wants to ease monetary policy, it injects liquidity into the system by buying government securities, such as U.S.

Treasury bills. With more money available in the system, interest rates come down and there is more money available to be lent out. If the Fed wants to tighten policy, it reverses the procedure.

The problem is, the Fed can't force its nominal benchmark interest rate below 0%. The odds increase that an economy falls into what Keynes called a "liquidity trap." When interest rates reach zero, there is essentially no difference between interest-bearing securities and money. So, even if the central bank creates more money in the banking system, banks may just hold on to it rather than take the risk of lending it out, since the returns are about the same but the risks are very different. "And if there's one lesson of history that screams out for attention, it's the lack of policy traction that typically occurs in such a climate," says Stephen Roach of Morgan Stanley. "Central banks, in particular, have had a terrible track record in curing deflation. The world in the 1930s and Japan in the 1990s are grim reminders of what happens when the authorities end up pushing on that proverbial string." [19]

The Risks of Not Dealing with Worker Insecurity

There are a lot of concerns surrounding deflation. The Fed is still figuring out how to cope—if at all—with deflationary pressures. But the problem is not the price level, however. No, the difficulty for everyone is adjusting to an intensely competitive environment that is reflected in prices. Right now, many workers are understandably worried about their living standards, since they're bearing the brunt of creative destruction. The federal and state government safety net is woefully inadequate for the new economy. The risk is that job insecurity will lead to trade protectionism, a policy that will inevitably backfire. Meeting the challenge of the new economy will demand investments in open borders, as well as in education, universal pension, and health care.

CHAPTER 6

THE GOAL OF PRICE STABILITY

"Papa, what's money?"

The abrupt question had such immediate reference to the subject of Mr. Dombey's thoughts, that Mr. Dombey was quite disconcerted.

"What is money, Paul?" he answered. "Money?"

"Yes," said the child, laying his hands on the elbows of his little chair, and turning the old face up toward Mr. Dombey's. "What is money?"

Mr. Dombey was in a difficulty. He would have liked to give him some explanation involving the terms circulating-medium, currency, depreciation of currency, paper, bullion, rates of exchange, value of precious metals in the market, and so forth; but looking down at the little chair, and seeing what a long way down it was, he answered: "Gold and silver, and copper. Guineas, shillings, half-pence. You know what they are?"

"Oh yes, I know what they are," said Paul. "I don't mean that, Papa. I mean what's money after all?"

—DICKENS

THE HISTORY OF MONEY AND FINANCE LONG predates the rise of capitalism. Most historians credit the 7th-century B.C. Lydian cities of the Aegean for introducing the first standardized coins, an alloy of gold and silver stamped with an official seal to guarantee weight and purity. The systematic use of loans goes even further back. Sumerian documents from around 3000 B.C. show loans were made with grain and metal as collateral, sometimes carrying interest. The common rate of interest for a loan of barley was 33⅓% a year and for a loan of silver 20%.[1] The integrity of the Athenian silver "owl" made it the most acceptable coin for trade and finance in the Mediterranean region for over 600 years. Leather money was used as banknotes in 2nd-century China, and the kingdom's mandarins invented paper money in the 9th century. Until the last third of the 20th century, except in times of national emergency, paper money was usually backed by some sort of commodity, with gold and silver the most common.

Economists look at money in two ways: as a standard for exchange and as a measure of value. "Money is a sort of medium or mean; for it measures everything and consequently measures among other things excess of defect, e.g., the number of shoes which are equivalent to a house or a meal," wrote the Greek philosopher Aristotle. "As a builder then is to a cobbler, so must so many shoes be to a house or a meal; for otherwise there would be no exchange or association. But this will be impossible, unless the shoes and the house and the meal are in some sense equalized. Hence arises the necessity of a single universal standard of measurement, as was said before. This standard is in truth the demand for mutual services, which holds society together."[2]

The same calculus holds for different national currencies. For example, in the San Francisco melting pot of the 1850s, the English shilling, the American quarter dollar, the French franc, the Mexican double real, Indian rupees, German and Dutch guilders and florins, and the coins of Latin America and elsewhere were circulating and widely accepted.[3] Banks, investment banks, hedge funds, pension funds, mutual funds, and corporate treasury departments trade trillions of dollars' worth of yen, euros, pesos, and other currencies every day on the global foreign exchange markets. Exchange is easy so long as buyers and sellers agree on the relative worth of these different national currencies.

Economists have a fairly strict definition of money. But in popular culture, money means much more than a measuring rod and means of exchange. It represents income, wealth, and status. So let's take a look at some other meanings of money.

We pay our bills with money we get from working. The typical American family is constantly juggling a mortgage, credit-card debt, and living expenses while trying to set aside some money for college education, emergencies, and retirement. Indeed, one way to look at personal finance is technical: How much cash is coming in, and how much money is going out? Should we buy a term insurance policy or whole life? Should we participate in the flexible spending account at work? What mutual funds should we put our retirement savings in? How should we crunch numbers to guesstimate how much we'll have in our golden years?

The most important meaning of money is trust. Wall Street deal makers aren't kidding—if they want to stay in business—when they say, "My word is my bond." The Latin derivation of *credit* means "to believe, to trust." The dollar bill in your pocket or wallet is backed by the full faith and credit of the federal government. The German philosopher Georg Simmel believed money tied modern society together. The money economy allows for the proliferation of needs, wants, objects, and cultural creations, giving us a degree of unprecedented choice in determining who we are and what we are, how we define ourselves and our community. At the same time, money and what it buys can control us, leading to a mindless, empty pursuit of wealth and material objects. Money is an abstract expression of community, but instead of having to know and trust a business rival, an anonymous seller, a company on the other side of the continent, we can trust money, a stable medium of exchange and a store of value.[4]

In other words, money affects and reflects our behavior and relations. To Karl Marx, money symbolized the exploitation by capitalists of the proletariat. To Max Weber, money encouraged rational thought about efficiency and trade-offs. For F. Scott Fitzgerald, money is success and power. "The very rich are different from you and me," said Fitzgerald. The wealthy have fewer constraints on their impulses and whims than the rest of us. Billionaires like Bill Gates, Warren Buffett, Larry Ellison, Michael Dell, Jeffrey Bezos, Barbara and Anne Cox Chambers, Oprah Winfrey, and Maurice Greenberg can buy luxuries, social status, good health care, the best private education, a seat at the table with the president of the United States—with plenty left over for heirs and philanthropy.

With rare exceptions, money affects our sense of worth and well-being far beyond putting a roof over our head and food on the table. Most employees judge much of their career success and their job performance through pay levels and pay raises. We associate higher prices with increased value, too, whether it's the value of an Ivy League education over a public university or a luxury six-cylinder car with leather interior compared to a four-cylinder compact with cloth-covered seats.

Money is deeply intertwined in everyday life. The calculus of money and the market, such as cost-benefit analysis and the risk and reward trade-off, are commonplace. Deregulation and privatization have placed market prices and market competition at the center of many public and quasipublic enterprises, from private prisons to waste collection. The market has spread into the professions like law and medicine. The professions had long been shielded from wide-open competition by a set of guild rules and norms that limited the supply of practitioners (hence high incomes) while frowning on practices routine in business. For instance, the 1930s-era Glass-Steagall Act barred commercial banks from investment banking. Pinstripe deal makers at Morgan Stanley, Kuhn, Loeb, Goldman Sachs, and other premier investment banking houses didn't have to worry about banks cutting in on their lucrative merger and acquisition business or competing to issue corporate equity and debt. No more. Commercial bankers and their high-priced lawyers chipped away at the Glass-Steagall prohibitions in the 1970s, 1980s, and early 1990s, as did aggressively avaricious investment banks, until the government changed the law and encouraged greater competition.

Money prices are the "ball bearings on which all spin," says John Julius Sviokla, a partner at the consulting firm Diamond Technology Partners. The price a company charges is the culmination of every decision made along the line, from the cost of raw materials to the cost of borrowed money to wages paid to workers. Many prices are fleeting, adjusting swiftly to changes in supply and demand, preferences and expectations. Some prices are remarkably stable for long periods of time.

Financial history is one of ongoing innovation that has aided commerce within and between regions of the world. Early civilization metal coins were far more efficient than barter; the establishment of the Bank of England in late 17th–century England encouraged trade; innovations like vendor shares, preference shares, and debentures increased the amount of capital flow for building railroads in the 19th century; the stateless Eurobond market in the 1960s met the capital needs of multinational corporations; the alchemy of securitization in the 1970s gave investors access to home mortgages; the derivatives revolution of the past two decades has allowed companies to manage their commercial and financial risks better than before.

Considering the stakes, is it any wonder that central bankers and economists worship at the altar of price stability? Trusting that a currency will hold its value, that a dollar today will be worth a dollar tomorrow, a year from now, or in 10 years, encourages trade and investment, planning and risk taking. Here is the great economist John Maynard Keynes on stable money in a capitalist society:[5]

[The economy] cannot work properly if the money . . .
assume[d] as a stable measuring rod, is undependable.

> Unemployment, the precarious life of the worker, the
> disappointment of expectation, the sudden loss of
> savings, the excessive windfalls to individuals, the
> speculator, the profiteer—all proceed, in large measure,
> from the instability of the standard of value. It is often
> supposed that the costs of production are threefold . . .
> labor, enterprise, and accumulation. But there is a fourth
> cost, namely, risk; and the reward of risk-bearing is one
> of the heaviest, and perhaps the most avoidable, burden
> on production. . . . [T]he adoption by this country and
> the world at large of sound monetary principles, would
> diminish the wastes of Risk, which consume at present
> too much of our estate.

Indeed, Keynes is wrongly associated with a tolerance for inflation.
He was an eloquent and ardent believer in price stability.[6]

> Thus, Inflation is unjust and Deflation is inexpedient.
> . . . But it is not necessary that we should weigh one evil
> against the other. It is easier to agree that both are evils
> to be shunned. The Individualistic Capitalism of today
> . . . presumes a stable measuring-rod of value, and cannot
> be efficient—perhaps cannot survive—without one.

The rise and fall of empires, expanding trade and economic
stagnation, and periods of intense innovations and brutal social cata-
clysms, all can be traced through changes in the overall value of
money and the reliability of credit, through the swings in inflation
and deflation. Society starts breaking down when trust in money
deteriorates. Venal Roman emperors tried to maintain their lavish
lifestyle and support an enormous bureaucracy by debauching the
currency, but eventually hyperinflation helped bring down the
empire. The poverty and social suffering in the deflationary 1930s
gave ideologues an opening, such as Hitler in Germany and Father

Coughlin in the United States, the anti-Semitic radio evangelist and his fascist politics. Faith in institutions and leaders declined during the Great Inflation of the 1970s. The inflation rate is treated as "a barometer of the economic and social health of a nation," says Robert Shiller, an economist at Yale University whose research shows that people pay close attention to the inflation rate. "High inflation is perceived as a sign of economic disarray, of a loss of basic values, and a disgrace to the nation, and embarrassment before foreigners," he adds.[7]

Changes in the price level play a critical role in the policy memory of a nation. The catastrophic policies of the Federal Reserve in the 1930s are inexplicable without considering Germany's hyperinflation after World War I. The reparations imposed on Germany by the victor nations were impossible for the new German government to meet, so the Weimar Republic eventually resorted to printed money. The German gold mark was worth 4.2 to the dollar in 1914. At the end of the war the paper mark—no longer linked to gold—was 14 to the dollar. By July 1922, it had fallen to 493 to the dollar; by January 1923, to 17,792, peaking shortly afterward at 4.2 billion to the dollar. The economic and social upheaval helped pave the way for Hitler's rise to power. In a talk given in 1978, economic historian Charles Kindleberger noted that the world remains troubled by the German memory of the hyperinflation of 1922–23 and the equivalent British paranoia about the unemployment of 1925–29, "fifty year old memories which play strong roles in shaping current macroeconomic policies."[8]

Price Stability

Of course, in a complex economy like America, some prices are always going up, some are flat, and others are heading lower. Price changes for particular goods and services largely reflect shifts in a

central concept of economics: supply and demand. Prices for gasoline, diamonds, drugs, Shaker furniture, taxicabs, and skilled labor
can surge if demand increases or supply shrinks, and vice versa. Now,
the phrase "supply and demand" brings a chill to many a survivor of
an Economics 101 course in college, manipulating supply and
demand curves, and calculating the elasticity of consumer demand
and business supply.

But if you think about it, most of us have a pretty sophisticated
understanding of supply and demand in the ordinary business of
life. Hot new cars typically go for well over the invoice price as
demand outstrips supply. Models that are showing their age sell at a
substantial discount to the invoice price. Home owners pay a premium to live in neighborhoods with good public schools and quality
of life, such as Milburn in New Jersey or the Mac-Grove neighborhood in St. Paul, Minnesota. California's glut of grapes allowed
winemaker Fred Franzia to create the varietal Two-Buck Chuck,
which sells for between $1.99 and $3.50 a bottle. (Okay, sometimes
you get exactly what you pay for.)

More important, if your child has grown up faster than you
thought possible and is now considering where to go to college,
you're well aware of the rising cost of a college sheepskin. The
demand for educated workers exceeds the supply. Ideas and skills
matter more than brawn and endurance. Here's just one of many
possible measures: The average annual earnings of men from 25 to
34 with a four-year college degree are about 60% greater than the
earnings of men with a high school diploma or GED. The comparable figure for women is 95%. In 1980 the earnings gap was 19% for
men and 52% for women.[9]

In the 1960s, War on Poverty advocates traveled the back roads
of Appalachia, among the nation's poorest regions. It's still economically depressed. When documentary producer John Biewen visited
eastern Kentucky in the late 1990s, he noted that reports of a soaring stock market and low unemployment seemed from another
country. Yet the value of a college education was well understood.[10]

For instance, Janet and Wilbur Wallen got married 20 years ago when he was 17 and she was 13, and they have two children, ages 12 and 14. Both have little education, and he worked at a truck assembly plant for $8.30 an hour. Her 12-year-old wants to get married at 18. Janet takes a deep breath:

> There ain't no way you can get married at the age of 18 and think that you can go through college, get a job, and support a family, and get your own home and everything else. You can't do that. That's what Mommy and Daddy's been a-trying to tell youn's. You get your education and everything, then you can get you a woman. Other than that, if you don't go through all of that, then you ain't gonna have nothin'. And you know it.

Wilbur agrees with his wife: "That's why I'm trying to get him and his brother to go on through college," he says. "Try to get 'em a good job where they can make a comfortable living, without having to get out and rake and scrape to pay the bills. Where they don't have to kill theirself like I have all my life."

The demand for a college degree has been so great that college tuition and fees have been rising at an 8% average annual rate for more than 30 years, pushing the cost of attending college, including tuition, fees, room and board, to around $86,000 for students graduating from a four-year public university in 2008 and $157,000 for a comparable private institution. That's before adding in four years of lost wages while earning a degree.

In sharp contrast, deflation is a way of life in high tech. Consumers are accustomed to the rhythm of a steep price tag for the latest gizmo marketed to the tech-savvy, followed by steep price cuts as the product is sold to the masses. Bay area reporter Mike Langberg took a nostalgic journey through his newspaper library and pulled out an ad for Fry's Electronics for Friday, May 23, 1997, and compared it to a similar Fry's ad for Friday, May 23, 2003. Here's what he found:[11]

- A 2.1-gigabyte hard drive for $179 in 1997; a 200-gigabyte hard drive—100 times bigger—for $139 in 2003.
- A 27-inch color TV went for $249 in 1997; it was $129 in 2003.
- A digital camera with 76,800 pixels of resolution was $199 in 1997; a digital camera with 1 million pixels was $97 in 2003.
- A Sony desktop computer with a 200-megahertz processor, 32 megabytes of random access memory (RAM), a 3.8-gigabyte hard drive, and a CD-ROM drive cost $2,199 in 1997; a Sony desktop PC with a 2.4-gigahertz processor, 256 megabytes of RAM, an 80-gigabyte hard drive, a DVD recorder, and a CD-ROM drive was $799 in 2003.

Of course, there were many tech products for sale in 2003 that didn't exist commercially for the mass market in 1997.

So, when economists talk about price stability, they're discussing the overall price level such as the consumer price index. The classic economic textbook on my bookshelf at work defines inflation as a rise in the general price level. Deflation is a fall in the general price level.

Now, what is the primary cause of inflation or deflation? Pick up any modern economics book and it will cite Nobel laureate Milton Friedman's famous proposition that "substantial inflation is always and everywhere a monetary phenomenon." The same goes for deflation. Inflation stirs when too much money is chasing too few goods, and not because the price of oil is up. As powerful U.S. Steel president Roger Blough quipped in the 1960s, "Steel prices cause inflation like wet sidewalks cause rain." Prices fall when too little money pursues too many goods, and not because Dell has sparked a price war among personal computer makers.

No, it takes substantial and sustained change in the money supply to bring about inflation or deflation. That's why a majority of economists have dismissed the prospect of deflation in a modern industrial economy. If the overall price level starts to fall, say, at a −1%

or −2% rate, all the government has to do to reverse the price decline is print more money. Milton Friedman suggested in the 1960s that a "helicopter drop of money" would solve deflation. The solution was tongue-in-cheek, but he was quite serious about the underlying observation. Charles Whelan, author of *The Naked Economist*, facetiously recommended he would solve deflation by giving every member of Congress $100 million of freshly minted bills to hand out to constituents. On a more serious note, Ben Bernanke, a leading scholar of the Great Depression and a Fed governor, said, "By increasing the number of dollars in circulation, or by even credibly threatening to do so, the U.S. government can also reduce the value of the dollar in terms of goods and services, which is equivalent to raising prices of those goods and services. We conclude that under a paper money system, a determined government can always generate higher spending and hence positive inflation."[12]

Inflation, sure. It's the modern disease. But deflation? No way.

Yet we've seen that deflation is a global economic force to be reckoned with. Sociologist Daniel Bell tells the cautionary story of how Austria's Prince Klemens von Metternich, the leading political leader on the Continent, made a classic mistake at the Congress of Vienna in 1815. Metternich's primary policy goal was to prevent France's armies from overrunning Europe again, as it had under Napoleon. What he did not see was that Germany was about to become a new and far more potent threat to the established order. Similarly, in their preoccupation with leaning and lecturing against the risk of inflation, policy makers didn't recognize that deflation was no longer confined to the moldy dustbin of the past.[13]

Measuring the Price Trend

Defining price stability isn't easy. It's increasingly hard to do in an economy where a growing fraction of overall economic value reflects intellectual insight and creative activity. How do you measure the price of ideas? Concepts are different from bars of steel, but both can have an economic value. Still, most economists believe that price stability translates into measured overall price increases of 1% to 2% a year. Some economists believe in zero inflation, and a few persuasively say that price stability requires mild deflation. It's not exactly a scientific answer, but price stability lies somewhere between 2% inflation and 2% deflation.

Let's take a look at the CPI. Statisticians at the Bureau of Labor Statistics calculate the CPI by tabulating price quotes on about 80,000 goods and services collected in 87 urban areas and from some 23,000 retail and service businesses. Data on rents come from 50,000 landlords or tenants. The numbers are adjusted in mathematically sophisticated ways to smooth out the series and to take into account quality improvements, among other things. Yet despite its breadth and consistency, the CPI has several well-recognized problems that may lead to the index overstating the rate of inflation—or understating the rate of deflation. The main issues are taking account of quality improvements, and capturing the impact of new technologies, substitution bias, and outlet bias.

An overall price measure should adjust for advances in quality. It's not that difficult for economists to capture and compare price differences of aluminum ingot, rolled steel, and cotton broad-woven fabric. The products are roughly similar over long periods of time. But it's extremely challenging to account for the impact of quality improvements in numerous existing products. Mervyn King, deputy governor of the Bank of England, notes that a record player in the department store giant Harrods cost 11 pounds for a hand-cranked machine with poor sound quality in 1910. A new record player goes on the Internet for 39 pounds. So, ignoring quality changes, the price of a record player has gone up 3.5 times in almost a hundred years. But ignoring quality changes vastly overstates the price increase, and that's before even mentioning that record players are out of date and most people buy CD players.[14]

The CPI struggles to incorporate the impact of new technologies that attract a lot of consumer dollars and affect our quality of life such as personal computers, cell phones, and microwave ovens. The CPI also misses some important shifts in consumer spending patterns. One such difficulty is called substitution bias. The CPI assumes that the market basket of goods and services that households buy doesn't change very quickly. But consumers are sensitive to price changes. They tend to buy less of an item that is rising in price and more if prices are falling. A classic example is consumers going to the supermarket and loading up on chicken when the price of beef goes up, or filling the basket with apples rather than oranges because apples are suddenly cheaper. Outlet bias is another issue. Many of us bought our CDs at a classic record store in the early 1990s. But by the late 1990s, you could buy a CD for $17 at a local record store or you could go to discount behemoth Wal-Mart and pick it up for $12. Guess where more and more people bought their CDs? At Wal-Mart or some other giant discount store. The same goes with toys.

Taken altogether, economists guesstimate that measurement issues add up to the CPI overstating inflation between 0.5 percentage points and 1.5 percentage points. Now, that gap isn't all that meaningful if inflation is actually running somewhere around 3%. But it matters a great deal when the economy is weak, and while government statisticians report that the CPI is growing at 1%, it may actually be closer to zero—or even negative.

The Fed

Currency crises were common in America between the end of the Civil War and the founding of the Federal Reserve in 1913. Monetary reform, meaning how to end deflation and banking panics, dominated political debates during that 50-year period.

The U.S. federal government had gained control over the nation's currency during the Civil War by issuing "greenbacks," essentially small-denomination non-interest-bearing government bonds. The government redeemed greenbacks 15 years after the war ended. The Confederate dollar was worthless, of course, wiping out capital holdings in many parts of the South. The sound money camp believed in the United States joining the gold standard, which would ensure the value of a dollar over the long haul. But in the short term, prices could be quite volatile, and the automatic workings of the gold standard prevented government from making adjustments to counter adverse shocks such as a financial panic. The political agitation for a bimetallic standard of both gold and silver that would have eased price pressures on many sectors of the economy was fierce. The political flashpoint was the "Crime of '73." Congress omitted the silver dollar from the list of coins to be minted, and three years later conspiracy theories fueled populist rage against the gold standard.

Competition among American banks was wide open, which was fitting for a frontier nation. Both national and state chartered banks operated without a central bank. The First Bank of the United States, chartered by Congress in 1791, did act like a central bank, but its charter wasn't renewed 20 years later by a federal government suspicious of centralized power. The Second Bank of the United States was created in 1816 when the U.S. government was broke following the War of 1812. Its charter ran out in 1836, and President Andrew Jackson vetoed its reauthorization. Jackson was no fan of the Second Bank, partly for what it represented. According to historian John Steele Gordon, the frontiersman Jackson detested the "monied aristocracy of the Eastern Seaboard, and those who dealt in paper—like bankers—rather than real wealth like land and manufacturing. The symbol of the monied aristocracy was the Second Bank. Getting rid of the national debt and the Second Bank would strike a blow against the financial aristocracy and for the self-made entrepreneur." [15]

Financial panics were commonplace. Domestic and international speculators funded innovation booms that promised investors enormous potential returns and rapid economic growth—investments such as the canals and the railroads. When the boom went bust as the more optimistic forecasts turned out to be wrong, money fled the capital markets, credit contracted, and banks failed as nervous depositors lined up to get their money. There was no central bank to act as a lender of last resort during financial crisis or to moderate the swings in the money supply.

The lack of a central bank was considered a sign of American financial backwardness. A central bank could support the economy during capitalism's inevitable downturns. Here's how the National Monetary Commission of 1912 looked at the American banking system.[16]

> The methods by which our domestic and international credit operations are now conducted are crude, expensive and unworthy of an intelligent people. . . . The unimportant part which our banks and bankers take in financing of our foreign trade is disgraceful to a progressive nation. . . . The disabilities from which our producers suffer in our foreign trade also apply largely to domestic transactions.

Still, there were some advantages to America's wildly competitive banking system and securities markets that grew up during the 19th century. It proved remarkably adept at funding innovation. For instance, growth drivers based on new technologies, transportation innovations, and the opening of the West were found in the United States as well as in Canada, Mexico, Brazil, Argentina, and other parts of the New World. Yet only America had a vibrant stock market and an intensely competitive banking system. That financial system paved the way for a huge flow of investment capital from Europe to America. "The U.S. financial system was so good that the assets it generated appealed to foreigners," says Richard Sylla, an economic historian at New York University Stern School of Business. "The U.S. was the most successful emerging market ever."[17]

Nevertheless, there was growing protest against destabilizing swings in prices and an agreement that price stability was desirable. The great American economist Irving Fisher described twenty-eight 19th-century proposals made by legislators and economists for a monetary standard based on a price index.[18] Commission after commission was formed to study monetary reform, from the Jones Commission of 1876 to the Pujo Committee of 1912. What turned proposals for a central bank into a reality was the legendary panic of 1907, among the most dramatic moments in American financial history.

The economy boomed in the early 1900s. The demand for credit was enormous. Corporate America was in the midst of one of the largest merger and acquisition waves in its history as financiers tried to stem ruinous price competition in industry after industry. Financial speculation was rampant, much of it conducted through trust companies. These were state-chartered financial institutions for managing wills, estates, and trust funds. Like commercial banks, the trusts accepted deposits and made loans, but weren't required to set aside reserves to back their portfolio. They were ideal financial vehicles for speculators.

The economy slowed in 1906 and 1907. Money drained out of the United States as Britain and Germany hiked interest rates to fund their imperialist wars. Investors were also unsettled by the Roosevelt administration's attacks on big business and big money. The trigger point for the panic was the unraveling of a scheme by speculators F. Augustus Heinze and Charles W. Morse through various trust companies to corner the stock of United Copper Company. Depositors rushed to take their money out of the trusts, and bank and businesses failed around the country.

To end the severe credit crunch, Wall Street and Washington turned to the legendary financier J. P. Morgan. The 70-year-old

Morgan established himself in the library in his New York house. The U.S. Treasury, European investors, commercial banks, John D. Rockefeller, and others put enormous financial resources at Morgan's disposal to stem the panic. Morgan and his allies kept confronting new problems throughout the two-week panic. The last maneuver involved a final $25 million loan provided by the trust companies. Morgan invited reluctant trust company presidents into his ornate library. Eventually, Morgan put paper and pen into the hand of Edward King, leader of the New York trusts, saying, "Here's the place, King. And here's the pen." The deal was signed and the panic was over. "The 1907 panic persuaded many skeptics that the country needed a central bank and couldn't rely upon the theatrics of aging tycoons any longer," says Ron Chernow, author of *The House of Morgan*. The Federal Reserve Board, America's central bank, was created in 1913.[19]

But price stability proved elusive. The deflation of the Great Depression was the institution's darkest hour, followed by the Great Inflation of the 1970s. Yet along the way, the Fed learned how to move closer to achieving the long-sought goal of price stability. And, in a world of paper money, constantly struggling to achieve price stability means, in practice, giving a deflationary bias to the currency.

CHAPTER 7

"Bad" Deflations

The great and often passionate interest that
is evoked by practical questions relating to
money and its value, can only be explained
by the fact that the monetary system of a
people reflects all that a people wants, all that
it suffers, all that it is; as well as by the fact
that a people's monetary system is an
important influence on its economy and on
the fate of society in general.

—JOSEPH SCHUMPETER

 THE UNITED STATES PRICE HISTORY IN THE 20TH
century is dominated by two major traumas: the
Great Deflation of the 1930s and the Great
Inflation of the 1970s. The former was an
unprecedented economic cataclysm for an industrial economy that nearly destroyed faith in capitalism and democratic freedoms. The fallout from the latter, while
far less severe than the Depression, threatened the fabric of everyday
economic vitality and trust in society's major institutions.

The Federal Reserve made major monetary mistakes that
could and should have been avoided in both cases. These episodes
reinforce Milton Friedman's dictum that substantial inflation and
substantial deflation are a monetary phenomenon that is always

present everywhere, in ancient times, emerging markets, capitalist societies, communist regimes, and so on. The lessons from these policy errors still strongly influence the Fed today.

Yet central bank incompetence isn't a sufficient explanation for major mistakes in policy. The Federal Reserve wasn't stacked with evil people or extremely stupid financiers in the 1930s or the 1970s. Decision makers and their advisors were mostly smart, ambitious, highly successful, and eager to do the right thing. Alan Meltzer, author of *A History of the Federal Reserve,* noted during an interview at the Federal Reserve Bank of Minnesota that "they did what many so-called sensible people at that time would have done. That is, it wasn't that they were chicane or evil, or that they wanted to destroy the country or that they had peculiar notions about what their responsibility was," he said. "They were acting in the way that most people acted at the time."[1]

No, delving into the basic question of why eventually leads to putting central bank decisions into the context of an overall economic, social, and intellectual system that justified a set of policy responses. As John Maynard Keynes put it in one of the most famous passages in economics:

The ideas of economists and political philosophers, both when they are right and when they are wrong, are more powerful than is commonly understood. Indeed, the world is ruled by little else. Practical men, who believe themselves to be quite exempt from any intellectual influences, are usually the slaves of some defunct economist. Madmen in authority, who hear voices in the air, are distilling their frenzy from some academic scribbler of a few years back. . . . Sooner or later, it is ideas, not vested interests, which are dangerous for good or evil.[2]

The Great Depression

The statistics that define the Great Depression are still unbelievable more than seven decades later. The U.S. economy fell by a third from the middle of 1929 to the first few months of 1933—10 times more than the average post–World War II decline. Defaults and debt delinquencies were commonplace among business, home owners, farmers, and state and local governments. More than 9,000 banks failed between 1930 and 1933, which is about a third of the banks that were open for business in 1929. Business investment collapsed. The Dow Jones Industrial Average fell from a height of 386.10 in September 1929, bottoming out at 41.22 in July 1930. The Radio Corporation of America, the high-tech darling of the 1920s, peaked at a high of $549 a share in 1929 and dropped all the way back down to a few bucks a share. A quarter of the workforce was unemployed. Some regions were hit even harder, such as the respective 50% and 40% unemployment rates in the manufacturing centers of Detroit and Chicago. Some 120,000 of New England's 280,000 textile mill hands were out of work by the end of 1930. African-American unemployment rates were about 50% higher than for whites. The overall price level plunged by a third, with many sectors of the economy devastated by price declines far greater than that, especially agriculture.[3]

These figures only hint at the social distress and personal tragedies of the era. Breadlines snaked around city blocks. Shantytowns called Hoovervilles sprang up on city outskirts. Millions and millions of families sank into appalling poverty. Here's how poet and activist John Beecher recalled the early years of the depression:[4]

> I had my first job in the steel mills, back in the Twenties.
> You could say that depression commenced in the town,
> Ainsley, Alabama, a steel mill suburb of Birmingham.
> We had the first bank to go bust in the early days of the

depression. All the workingmen trusted the banker. I remember an old group of Italians, who had been brought over from Italy in the 1890s to work in this mill. They, like the blacks and poor whites, were kept at common labor all their lives and were never allowed to rise. Yet they trusted this banker with their life savings, which were swept away in that bank crash. In '32 the plant was shut down and stayed shut for years. It became a ghost town, never quite recovered.

Farmers were hard hit. Agricultural prices declined by 56% between 1929 and 1932. The number of farms in foreclosure soared, and by 1932 over half of all farm debts were in default. John Steinbeck memorably captured the trauma of tenant farmers driven off the land by big banks and big business.[5]

> The owners of the land came onto the land, or more often a spokesman for the owners came. . . . The tenants, from their sun-beaten dooryards, watched uneasily when the closed cars drove along the fields. . . . Some of them hated the mathematics that drove them, and some were afraid, and some worshiped the mathematics because it provided a refuge from thought and from feeling. If a bank or finance company owned the land, the owner man said, The Bank—or the Company—needs— wants—insists—must have—as though the Bank or the Company were a monster, with thought and feeling, which had ensnared them.

The severe price deflation of the Great Depression damaged economic activity through several channels. One way is through higher "real" interest rates. During the expansion of the 1920s, generous credit fueled a real estate boom, business investment in new technologies and techniques, and a bull market in stocks. The 1920s was an era of stable to low interest rates, with the yield on long-term government bonds declining from 5.32% in 1920 to 3.60% in 1929. Prime corporate bond yields went from 5.27% to 4.47% over the same time period. The consumer price index fell at an average annual rate of 1.8%, and the real rate of interest averaged about 3%. By one account, the real rate of interest surged during the Great Depression, averaging 5.9% in 1929, 8.2% in 1930, 15.5% in 1931, and 15% in 1932.[6]

Companies typically rely on some sort of borrowing to fund their investment, and with real interest rates at double-digit levels, it's hardly surprising that business investment collapsed. A similar story holds for households. Consumers went on a spending spree in the 1920s, especially for cars. Consumer debt doubled as a percent of personal income from 1918–20 to 1929. Family finances grew increasingly perilous, with work scarce and the cost of repaying debt ratcheting higher. Businesses and households drastically scaled back their activities because of impaired balance sheets and precarious finances. Often, bankruptcy was the only option for discharging debts.

As we saw earlier, deflation ominously interacts with wages, too. Economists consider nominal wages "sticky," since workers understandably dislike pay cuts. Employers are well aware that slashing wages leads to all kinds of morale and productivity problems. So, if the nominal wage level remains stable, the real wage employers hand out goes up with deflation. The higher cost of labor drives companies to lay off employees. Still, the real wage impact was probably less than the real interest rate effect during the Great Depression. Wages in some sectors of the economy, say, restaurants, are more flexible than in others, such as manufacturing. For instance, while real wages in manufacturing rose by an estimated 6% from 1929 to 1932, the real wage outside of the factory and mining sector declined by some 8%.[7]

The scary downward price spiral of the 1930s simultaneously reflected and contributed to the severity and magnitude of the Great

Depression. How much of the downturn is attributable to deflation? Charles T. Carlstrom and Timothy S. Furst, two economists at the Federal Reserve Bank of Cleveland, came up with a back-of-the-envelope calculation suggesting that the net effect of price deflation on the economy from 1929 to 1933 was about a third of the plunge in output. The exact percentage is unknowable, of course, but deflation was largely the result of a catastrophic collapse and not the cause of it.

What Caused the Great Depression?

Booms and busts are inevitable with capitalism—it is in the nature of the beast. The National Bureau of Economic Research, a non-profit organization and the official arbiter of the American business cycle, lists 16 downturns between 1854 and 1919. Deflations were commonplace whenever the economy turned down in the 19th and early 20th centuries. Indeed, during the short, sharp depression of 1920–21, prices fell by some 56% from mid-1920 to mid-1921, perhaps the steepest price plunge in U.S. history.

The question economists have long grappled with is what transformed a severe recession into the worst depression on record. The controversy over the 1930s has been fierce, fascinating, and illuminating. Among some well-known explanations: John Maynard Keynes blamed a collapse in business confidence and private investment in *The General Theory of Interest, Money, and Employment;* Milton Friedman and Anna Schwartz scorched an inept Federal Reserve; Peter Temin emphasized a collapse in consumer spending; Joseph Schumpeter argued the economy was plagued by "underconsumption" as highly productive business flooded the market with more goods than consumers had income; John Kenneth Galbraith's culprit was the bursting of an immense stock market bubble; Ben Bernanke stressed the impact of credit contraction; and Charles Kindleberger identified the worldwide fall in commodity prices.

Each of these interpretations resonates, and much of the economic debate has been over primacy—the stock market crash? the banking panics? a deflationary spiral?—rather than role. The answer is unusually important, however. Trying to understand the Great Depression is no abstract puzzle. No one wants to go through another era where a quarter of the workforce is out of work, or to create the kind of economic upheaval that gave a tragic opening to extremists like the Nazis in Germany.

One framework is especially illuminating for understanding the causes of the tragedy. It has emerged in recent years, and among the seminal contributors are Barry Eichengreen of the University of California, Berkeley; Peter Temin of the Massachusetts Institute of Technology; Jeffrey Sachs of Columbia University; and Michael Bordo of Rutgers University. The literature begins with the global nature of the depression. And as Eichengreen and Temin emphasize, that means putting the international gold standard and central banks at the core of the story.[8]

> The constraints of the gold-standard system hamstrung
> countries as they struggled to adapt during the 1920s
> to changes in the world economy. And the ideology,
> mentality and rhetoric of the gold standard led
> policymakers to take actions that only accentuated
> economic distress in the 1930s. Central banks continued
> to kick the world economy while it was down until it lost
> consciousness. . . . The modern literature on the Great
> Depression emphasizes mentality, discourse, mass
> politics, and the eclipse of the nation state.

The gold standard was much more than a system for managing exchange rates and ensuring stable currency values. It had evolved into a secular religion that gave coherence to the world economy and trust in financial transactions. The experience of the latter part of the 19th and early 20th centuries was that the gold standard played a vital role in the long economic boom of that period. Now, the gold standard had been discontinued during the First World War. But after the war, political and financial elites saw restoring the gold standard as critical for bringing back healthy international relations among war-weary nations. For instance, in 1918 the British government established the Cunliffe Commission, headed up by Lord Cunliffe, the former governor of the Bank of England, to make currency recommendations once the war was over. The final report made clear that the only acceptable choice was a return to gold: "The adoption of a currency not convertible to gold or other exportable gold is likely in practice to lead to over issue and so to destroy the measure of exchangeable value and cause a general rise in all prices and an adverse movement in the foreign exchanges."[9]

The Cunliffe Commission reflected the mentality of the gold standard. The mindset of policy makers limited their choice of what was possible. Abandoning the gold standard during peacetime would only lead to inflation, profligate government, and broken commercial contracts. The gold standard stood for everything that was good in society. Thrift. Sobriety. Civilization. International harmony. An international monetary system not backed by gold meant giving in to society's worst tendencies, the license of the mob, and the destruction of capital. The idea was so heretical that many elites couldn't even think of not rushing to reestablish the gold standard now that war was over.

That's why policy makers couldn't grasp that the world economy had changed in fundamental ways and actions taken to shore up the system had the exact opposite effect. The First World War changed the face of politics, especially in Europe. Before the Great War, a political, military, financial, and business elite dominated their nations, supported by the moneyed, property-owning middle class. But the Victorian and Edwardian eras disappeared after traditional elites lost credibility with their blundering into a war that is still largely inexplicable, as well as tolerating an unimaginable slaughter on the battlefield, from the battles for Ypres to the battle of the Somme. An estimated 10 million soldiers were killed, twice that seriously wounded, and casualties among civilians totaled some 30 million. Says Ronald Jepperson, professor of sociology at Tulsa University: "World War I shattered the European Old Regime, the aristocratic political order that had persisted into the 20th century. The elites that had thrust their populations into war were thoroughly discredited as well as demoralized."

The wartime mobilization of the population, coupled with the massive disruptions and widespread discontent, spawned populist movements of all colorations: liberal and soft socialist parties in the more democratic countries; autocratic nationalist parties (both left and right) in the more authoritarian ones. The opinion of working men and women could no longer be ignored following the enormous sacrifices of the war. Membership in unions grew. Socialist and communist parties attracted followers. Fascists competed for support among the same disillusioned masses. Agitation for the right to vote rapidly spread. There were substantial, if less extreme, effects in the United States as well. Women did gain the right to vote in 1919. Millions of young Americans from rural areas that served in the war migrated to cities for better jobs and a more exciting life following armistice. "In all cases, if in different ways," says Jepperson, " 'public opinion' was now in part mass opinion—the latter a new restraint upon policy-making, as well as a new source of power for would-be reformers and revolutionaries of all stripes."

Central banks are also critical to this accounting of the unprecedented collapse. Focusing on the United States, any analysis of the Great Depression today has to deal with Milton Friedman and Anna Schwartz's *A Monetary History of the United States, 1867–1960*. The authors argue that the Federal Reserve transformed a cyclical contraction into a depression. In essence, the Great Depression stems from a decline in the money supply. The public lost confidence in banks. Depositors wanted their money back. The money supply contracted. Bank deposits weren't being used to expand credit and economic activity but rather to meet the public's panicked need for cash. Incomes fell, economic activity plummeted, and more banks went out of business. Yet the Fed refused to break the cycle of fear by acting as the lender of last resort. "The experience was a tragic testimonial to the importance of monetary forces," write Friedman and Schwartz.[10]

> The drastic decline in the quantity of money during those years and the occurrence of a banking panic of unprecedented severity were not the inevitable consequences of other economic changes. They did not reflect the absence of power on the part of the Federal Reserve System to prevent them. Throughout the contraction, the System had ample powers to cut short the tragic process of monetary deflation and banking collapse. Had it used those powers effectively in late 1930 or even in early to mid-1931. . . . Such action would have eased the severity of the contraction and very likely would have brought it to an end at a much earlier date.

With the benefit of hindsight, it's unbelievable that the Fed would allow for the destruction of wealth, enterprise, and employment. Friedman and Schwartz strongly emphasize the ineptness of the Fed as well as a struggle for power between the Federal Reserve Bank of New York and the Federal Reserve Board in Washington, D.C. The scholars believe that had Benjamin Strong, the forceful head of the New York Fed, not died in 1928, he might have taken the kind of bold action necessary to stem the Depression's downward spiral. "The shift of power from New York to the other Banks might not have been decisive, if there had been sufficiently vigorous and informed intellectual leadership in the Board," write Friedman and Schwartz. "However, no tradition of leadership existed within the Board. It had not played a key role in determining the policy of the System throughout the twenties. . . . There was no individual Board member with Strong's stature in the financial community or in the Reserve System, or with comparable experience, personal force, or demonstrated courage.[11]

Eichengreen and other scholars agree that the Fed deserves considerable blame for the Great Depression. But in contrast to Friedman and Schwartz, they emphasize the rationality of the decisions made by the Fed in light of the dictates of the gold standard. When the Fed was confronted with an outflow of gold, as it was in the fall of 1931 and in early 1933, staying true to logic of the gold standard meant raising U.S. interest rates even though some 13 million Americans or about a quarter of the workforce was unemployed. The gold standard mechanism limited the freedom of central bankers to expand the money supply to encourage domestic demand because, horror of horrors, that could lead to inflation. Remember, this is at a time when prices were falling at an annual rate as high as 10%. "Policies were perverse because they were designed to preserve the gold standard, not employment," say Eichengreen and Temin.[12]

The mind-set of financial and policy elites sheds light on one of the most infamous statements about letting the Depression run its course without government interference: "Liquidate labor, liquidate stocks, liquidate the farmers, liquidate real estate," said Andrew Mellon, President Herbert Hoover's Treasury secretary. Following the boom of the 1920s, he believed the downturn would "purge the rottenness out of the system. High costs of living and high living will come down. People will work harder, live a more moral life. Values will be adjusted, and enterprising people will pick up the wrecks from less competent people." Sure, that's an easy perspective for one of the nation's wealthiest men to hold. The problem is, many of the best minds of the era also valued depressions as purgatives wiping away speculative excesses created during booms. The "depression is good for you" crowd included legendary economists like Joseph Schumpeter, Friedrich Hayek, and Lionel Robbins, according to a fascinating paper by Brad DeLong, economist at the University of California, Berkeley, and deputy assistant secretary in the Clinton administration's Treasury Department.[13]

Schumpeter was of the opinion that "depressions are not simply evils, which we might attempt to suppress, but . . . forms of something which has to be done, namely, adjustment to change." His contemporary, Lionel Robbins, wrote, "Nobody wishes . . . bankruptcies. Nobody likes liquidation as such. . . . [But] when the extent of mal-investment and over-indebtedness has passed a certain limit, measures which postpone liquidation only make matters worse."

These opinions were supported by the experience of the 19th century, which suggested that busts weren't all bad. Investment booms surrounded new technologies, but the return on investment is always uncertain. How many miles of canals should be dug? How many lines of railroads make competitive sense? Which city will grab enough business to justify building skyscrapers? Business entre-preneurs and financial speculators gambled, sometimes going too far, that excess capacity would be liquidated, creating conditions for another technology-led investment spree. Here's Brad DeLong on the pre–World War I business cycle:

There was uncertainty about the long run growth of the American economy, especially when settlement of the West is concerned. Railroads are sensitive to the growth of the regions they serve. Entrepreneurs did risk their fortunes and futures on their assessment of the quasi-rents to be earned from a particular line. Sometimes they guessed wrong: Jay Cooke and Co. failed because it had advanced more money for the construction of the Northern Pacific than it could recoup by selling Northern Pacific bonds. Its failure ushered in the panic of 1873 and the subsequent depression, which did not lift until five years had passed and construction resumed. Thus railroad booms and busts of the late nineteenth century are not inconsistent with a "liquidationist" perspective. When long run rates of growth are unstable,

investment for the future ought to be jagged, and ought
to see periods of rapid expansion coupled with periods of
quiescence and disinvestment.[14]

This isn't to say the liquidationists were right. Just that the
business cycle experience and the gold standard combined to drive
policy elites to take the wrong actions—turning a severe recession
into a Great Depression.

Gradually, however, the human and productive toll grew too
great and the political agitation too insistent to ignore. In 1931, 47
countries adhered to the gold standard; by the end of 1932, the only
major countries left were Belgium, France, Italy, the Netherlands,
Poland, Switzerland, and the United States. Britain abandoned its
commitment to gold in the fall of 1931. The United States went off
the gold standard in 1933 with the election of President Franklin
D. Roosevelt, who ignored the pleas of his predecessor, Herbert
Hoover, to stick with gold. The rest of the gold bloc countries had
abandoned the standard by the end of 1936. The nations that shook
off their "golden fetters" first were also first to leave the Great
Depression behind.

Could It Happen Again?

For most of the post–World War II era, the answer was no to the
question of whether another Great Depression could happen in a
modern industrial economy. One reason is that no politician today
would stand by while a quarter of the workforce went unemployed.
Another factor is that macroeconomists, determined not to allow
another depression, made real strides in understanding the business
cycle, the direction of employment, prices, and output. "Not only did
the Depression give birth to macroeconomics as a distinct field of
study, but also—to an extent that is not always fully appreciated—

the experience of the 1930s continues to influence macroeconomists' beliefs, policy recommendations, and research agendas," says Fed governor Ben S. Bernanke. "Macroeconomics was born as a distinct field in the 1940s, as part of the intellectual response to the Great Depression," adds Robert Lucas Jr., Nobel laureate and University of Chicago economist. "Its central problem of depression-prevention has been solved, for all practical purposes, and has in fact been solved for many decades." [15]

Deflation was also a problem of the past. Economists and central bankers believed they knew how to prevent deflation and, anyway, they were far more concerned about inflation. That's why mainstream forecasters missed Japan's journey into deflation. In the early 1990s, the idea of deflation was inconceivable. Yet Japanese prices of food, clothing, footwear, furniture, transportation, communication, housing rent, and durable goods have all registered gradual declines. Money wages were down in four out of the past five years. Joblessness is at record highs. Surveys show that deflation expectations are becoming ingrained among Japanese businesses and consumers—prices will keep falling, so why buy today when it will be cheaper tomorrow?

What went wrong? Japan is not in a depression. It's stuck in a deflationary stagnation. The Japanese central bank was timid in responding to deflationary pressures, even though it lowered short-term rates from around 8% in early 1991 to essentially zero at decade's end. Fiscal policy was also inept, with Japanese politicians preferring to dither rather than act boldly. The banking system was staggering under a tsunami of bad loans. To a number of economists, such as Paul Krugman of Princeton University and the *New York Times,* Japan had fallen into a "liquidity trap." He convincingly argues that rates were so low that conventional monetary policy techniques were incapable of reviving the economy. Other economists prefer to emphasize that the contraction of bank credit, or "credit crunch," was primary. Banks have been reluctant to lend out fresh money, considering all their bad loans and heightened regulatory scrutiny. Low productivity and barriers to competition in much of the Japanese economy are also blamed, especially with competition from Japan's Asian neighbors picking up.

There is some optimism that Japan is emerging from its long deflation. Japan's politicians now label deflation as problem number one. Monetary policy is getting more aggressive and creative. International pressure is growing for Japan to coordinate its fiscal and monetary policies to combat deflation. Still, the lesson most experts take from Japan's experience is the same lesson of the Great Depression: if demand is weak, and the financial system impaired, it's up to the fiscal and monetary authorities to pull out all the stops to prevent deflation from settling in. Certainly, the American Fed acted aggressively to counter deflation during the weak economy of 2000–2003.

But as we have seen, deflation can also reflect strong economic growth. The struggle for the Fed—and other central banks—will be to learn how to live with benign deflation and prevent bad deflation.

CHAPTER 8

THE GREAT INFLATION

> The trouble with paper money is that it
> rewards the minority that can manipulate
> money and makes fools of the generation that
> has worked and saved.
>
> —GEORGE GOODMAN

THE WIDELY SHARED FEAR AFTER THE END OF THE
Second World War was that America would sink
into another depression. Forecasters routinely
predicted a loss of millions of jobs, and a federal
survey suggested that more than half the nation's
soldiers expected an economic depression after
the war.[1]

Yet the years 1930 to 1945 mark one of the great divides
in U.S. history. The difference between the bleakness of the 1930s
and the plenty after the Second World War astonished contemporary observers. "The compilation of statistics might be extended
endlessly, but it would only prove repetitively that in every aspect
of material plenty America possesses unprecedented riches and that
these are very widely distributed among one hundred and fifty million American people," wrote historian David Potter in his 1954
book, *People of Plenty: Economic Abundance and the American Char-
acter.* "If few can cite the figures, everyone knows that we have,
per capita, more automobiles, more telephones, more radios, more

vacuum cleaners, more electric lights, more bathtubs, more super-markets and movie palaces and hospitals, than any other nation."[2]

Ah, those were the days. The economy flourished following demobilization from 1948 to 1967, a prosperity marred by only three mild recessions. In a golden era for America's industrial econ-omy, wages and incomes rose smartly, and the civilian unemploy-ment rate only breached 6% twice. The modern middle class came of age. Millions of Americans bought homes for the first time in places like Levittown, a suburb built on a potato field in Long Island for returning soldiers and their families, including my parents. Sol-diers, cops, firemen, and working- and middle-class folk moved into prefabricated homes that initially ranged in prices from $9,900 to $16,900 (about $80,000 to $135,000 in today's dollars). On the other coast, the Southern California beach and car lifestyle seized the nation's imagination. Luxury goods like refrigerators, televisions, and range-top stoves went mass market. The G.I. Bill opened the doors of elite colleges to returning soldiers. Agriculture became industrialized, and smokestack America thrived.

The mantra of big business, big government, and big labor was "never again." The basic idea for preventing another depression was to keep capitalist competition contained. Andrew Shonfield, the British scholar, began his 1965 book, *Modern Capitalism: The Changing Balance of Public and Private Power,* with a discussion of whether the new system could still be called capitalism, since the "economic order under which we now live and the social structure that goes with it are so different from what preceded them that it is misleading—so it is alleged—to use the word 'capitalism' to describe them."[3]

It was a triumph of policy that another depression didn't emerge. But the system of managed capitalism started running into trouble toward the end of the 1960s and into the 1970s. The rise of international competition. The Vietnam War. The oil shocks of the 1970s. The plunge in productivity. The hollowing out of American manufacturing. A series of currency crises. The defining economic problem was inflation, a rise in prices that was both the cause and effect of the breakdown of managed capitalism. By the late 1960s, almost four decades after the Great Depression, inflation took off, rising from almost 6% in 1970 to more than 14% in 1980. The unemployment rate doubled in the 1970s, jumping to about 8% in 1980 and 10% in 1982.

To be sure, the price trauma of the 1970s paled next to the deflation of the 1930s. Nevertheless, an upward price spiral shook society. Lawrence K. Roos, president of the Federal Reserve Bank of St. Louis, compared the battle against inflation to the struggle against communism in a talk to the 1980 graduating class at Westminster College, Fulton, Missouri:

> It was 34 years ago that Winston Churchill came to
> Westminster and warned his audience and the nation
> of an ominous threat to our peace and security by
> enemies from abroad. The course of world events in the
> intervening years has fully justified his concern. Today, I
> would warn you of a different threat of similar gravity—a
> threat that, in this instance, comes not from abroad but
> from within our own society. . . . The threat I would
> warn you of is accelerating inflation—a burden which
> our nation has endured for the past decade and which,
> unless appropriate counter-measures are promptly taken,
> is likely to have catastrophic economic, social, and
> political consequences in the years to come.[4]

Okay, there is more than a little hyperbole in those sentences. Yet there was Ronald Reagan at his 1981 inauguration address echoing the fears of a nation traumatized by inflation. "These United States are confronted with an economic affliction of great proportions. We suffer from the longest and one of the worst sustained inflations in our national history. It's distorting our economic decisions, penalizing thrift, and crushing the struggling young and the fixed income elderly alike. It threatens to shatter the lives of millions of our people."[5]

Clearly, inflation was the modern problem, and deflation faded into the history books. What happened? Once again, the Fed is to blame for much of the price mistake. To be sure, the central bank talked a good game against inflation. The reality is that under chairmen Arthur Burns and G. William Miller, the Fed ran an inept monetary policy that stoked the fires of inflation. By the end of the 1970s the Fed had little credibility internationally or domestically as an inflation-fighting central bank. The oft-stated goal of price stability was a joke, something Fed members had to say—they were central bankers after all—but didn't mean. Many economists believed the best that could be accomplished was to stabilize the inflation rate at around 10%, recalls Michael J. Boskin, head of the White House Council of Economic Advisors during the first Bush presidency.[6] Daniel Bell, the astute sociologist, observed in his 1976 book, *The Cultural Contradictions of Capitalism,* that "economic growth has been inextricably linked with inflation, and it seems unlikely that any democratic political economy can abolish its inflation without disastrous political consequences."

Yet a lack of good Fed leadership isn't enough of an explanation for the inflation of the 1970s. No, the economic and ideological backdrop of the time, especially memories of massive unemployment during the Great Depression, contributed to a tolerance of inflation that badly backfired. Economists were overconfident that they could manipulate the levers of fiscal and monetary policy with enough success to keep inflation contained at a stationary level, perhaps 3% or 5%. The runaway inflation of the 1970s also came as a surprise. After all, from 1800 to the present, peacetime inflation averaged 0.4% (excluding the inflations of the War of 1812, the Civil War, World War I, World War II, the Korean War, and the Vietnam War, and ignoring the Persian Gulf War), calculates Peter Bernstein.[7] "The best bet on inflation is a low number, by which we mean a number so low it has no effect on spending plans or longer-run decisions," says Bernstein. "That is the unimpeachable lesson of history." Adds Brad DeLong of the University of California, Berkeley: "It is the inflation of the 1970s that is the anomaly."[8]

Indeed, it was society's loathing of inflation that finally invigorated the Fed to combat it, setting the stage for the turn toward deflation 20 years later.

The Era of Managed Competition

A pillar of the post–Second World War economy was laid at the Mt. Washington Hotel, a white behemoth nestled at the foot of Mt. Washington, the highest peak in the Northeast. Representatives from 44 Allied nations and a neutral Argentina met in New Hampshire to plan for postwar economic stability. The Bretton Woods Conference included many of the world's leading international finance and economic experts, with the British delegation led by John Maynard Keynes and the Americans by Harry Dexter White, chief international economist at the U.S. Treasury. Instead of trying to re-create the classical gold standard, the conference settled on a modified gold standard based on stable, adjustable exchange rates pegged to the dollar that still gave government some flexibility. Foreign currencies were fixed in relation to the value of the dollar, and the dollar was convertible into gold at $35 an ounce.[9]

The new monetary regime dominated by America was designed to prevent beggar-thy-neighbor currency devaluations. It was also intended to limit the influence of financial speculators. Both devaluations and speculators were considered prime villains behind the turmoil of the previous three decades. Limiting speculative capital flows would help maintain international economic stability. The International Monetary Fund was established to lend temporary funds to countries facing exchange rate difficulties. The

World Bank (then called the Bank for Reconstruction and Development) was founded to make loans to developing countries.

Order was also brought to the American financial markets. For example, the Fed could control the interest rate paid on savings accounts. It could also set limits on borrowing for speculation. The Fed set margin requirements on loans taken out to purchase securities, and from 1963 to 1971 the rate was set at 65%. Long-time Wall Street economist Albert Wojnilower has called the American financial system of the time a well-run and orderly zoo.[10] The various species—banks, securities dealers, insurance companies, thrifts, and so on—were prevented (and protected) from competing with one another. The days of financiers like J. P. Morgan and Jacob Schiff dominating Corporate America through the "money trust" of interlocking directorships and financial institutions were past. The reputations of investment bankers, brokers, and speculators had been shattered by the 1929 crash and its aftermath while Corporate America was generating so much cash that it relied less and less on Wall Street's fund-raising prowess.

Big business developed a close relationship with government. Professional managers at giant firms like General Electric, U.S. Steel, IBM, Sears, and General Motors dominated cartel-like industries that shunned the anarchy of laissez-faire competition for a cozier existence that prevented ruinous price wars—that is, ruinous to corporate profits. American labor never achieved the same power at the table as European unions. Nevertheless, the percent of private-sector workers belonging to trade unions rose from 14.2% in 1935 to 37% in 1960.

Many more people were affected by the growth of large bureaucratic organizations that pursued predictability through planning. William Whyte's *The Organization Man*, an extraordinary work, captured and analyzed the society and culture of an economy dominated by such employees in government and business.[11] "Increasingly it will be recognized the mature corporation, as it develops, becomes part of the larger administrative complex associated with the state. In time the line between the two will disappear," wrote John Kenneth Galbraith in *The New Industrial State.* "The control by the mature corporation over its prices, its influence on consumer behavior, the euthanasia of stockholder power, the regulation by the state of aggregate demand, the effort to stabilize prices and wages, the role of publicly supported research and development, the role of military, space and related procurement, the influence of the firm on these government activities and the modern role of education are, more or less, accepted facts of life." [12]

Above all, the role of government in the economy expanded. The 19th-century laissez-faire ideal was for government to stay small and focus on essential public works, maintenance of law and order, and defense. Capital was protected at the expense of labor. No one really believed in laissez-faire anymore. It was too risky a policy. The postwar welfare state reached deep into the economy to tame capitalism and protect the worker. The public deeply mistrusted the market while believing the government was the solution to most problems. For instance, total government expenses as a share of America's GDP were a mere 8% in 1913 but soared to 21% in 1950 and 31% in 1973. The Employment Act of 1946 committed the federal government to maintaining a low unemployment rate, and the government actively intervened in the economy to keep growth strong. The new welfare state took some of the risk out of being out of work with unemployment insurance. Older Americans got a safety net through Social Security and federal public assistance created an income floor for the nation's poorest citizens. Medicare and Medicaid were added later on to take care of the health bills of the elderly and the poor, respectively. This was the era that still defines much of what most of us consider a good life: lifetime employment, company benefits, relationship banking, interest rate ceilings, and regulated public utilities.

Inflation, the Scourge of the Nation

The system of managed capitalism fell apart during the tumultuous 1970s. The rise in the price level during the Great Inflation robbed savings, battered stocks, savaged bonds, and chipped away at wages and corporate profits. During the 1973–74 bear market, stocks plunged by more than 40% before touching bottom, and the bond market suffered a 35% loss while the cost of living jumped some 20%.[13]

Business complained bitterly about rising cost pressures from land, labor, and materials. Inflation distorts the basics of business, rewarding companies skilled at financial engineering, delaying debt payments, and quickly collecting money rather than rewarding innovation and long-term investments. Their labor force was unhappy as pay raises fell behind the rate of inflation even as inflation drove millions of Americans into higher tax brackets.

Savers were savaged. The concept "a penny saved is a penny earned" became a bad joke. A person who put $10,000 in a savings account in 1965 would have had an account worth $18,000 in 1980. Problem is, after adjusting for inflation, the real value of $18,000 was only $8,000.[14] The living standards of retirees or anyone on a fixed income eroded fast. Investors shunned the stock and bond markets, the lifeblood of the economy. Economist William Melton recalls teaching an evening course for MBA students in Manhattan in the 1970s. Most of the students worked in the financial district, so they were reasonably sophisticated about money. Melton always polled his students on their preferred investments, and the students routinely favored stocks, bonds, and owner-occupied housing. Yet in 1979, when inflation was spiraling higher at a double-digit rate, the answers were very different. Out of a class of 60 students, two votes were cast for stocks and none for interest-bearing securities. A sizable number liked housing, but the best investments were considered gold and art—traditional hedges against inflation.[15] "Obviously, if society expects sustained inflation, few people will save (since the money will steadily lose value) or commit their money to long-term investments in bonds or equity shares," wrote sociologist Daniel Bell in 1976.[16]

Of course, not everyone loses with inflation. Farmers did well. So did anyone working in the oil and mineral industries. The middle class benefited for a while from inflation, mainly because home prices rapidly appreciated. Conventional wisdom among families and neighbors was to take on as big a mortgage as possible, since the bank or thrift was paid with depreciating dollars.

Still, inflation is widely perceived as a major problem when it stirs, an opinion shared by the Wall Street bond trader to the newly minted college graduate to the worker on the factory floor. The loathing of inflation stems from a number of sources. Inflation is perceived to lower living standards, reward speculation over thrift, and lead to economic and political chaos. Put it this way: No one likes the idea that the dollar bill in their pocket will be worth significantly less a year from now. A Gallup poll question asked since 1935 is, "What do you think is the most important economic problem facing this country today?" The percentage answering inflation was over 50% from 1973 to 1981, the high inflation years.[17]

The public buys into John Maynard Keynes's eloquent comment:

> Lenin is said to have declared that the best way to
> destroy the capitalist system was to debauch the
> currency. . . . As the inflation proceeds and the real value
> of the currency fluctuates wildly from month to month,
> all permanent relations between debtors and creditors,
> which form the ultimate foundations of capitalism,
> become so utterly disordered as to be almost
> meaningless, and the process of wealth-getting
> degenerates into a gamble and a lottery.[18]

Why did America's experience of low inflation come to an end in the late 1960s? Like understanding the Great Depression, a number of theories have emerged over the years. Some stories emphasize the role of union wage demands setting off an economy-wide wage-and-price spiral. Others point to the federal government's reckless pursuit of both guns and butter while waging the unpopular Vietnam War, followed by the oil embargo shocks imposed by the Organization of Petroleum Exporting Countries (OPEC). The tectonic shift from a highly productive industrial economy to a far less efficient service economy is a prime culprit, as well as a rising sense of entitlement among young and old alike in the richest nation in history. All of these narratives capture an element of the cumulative spiral in inflation. But like the Great Depression, the most profound causes of the Great Inflation lie with money and memory, compounded by a weak, hapless Fed.

The End of Managed Capitalism

The U.S. economy stood tall after World War II. It accounted for approximately 60% of the world output of manufacturing in 1950. Sounds good if you are an American. But the situation was unhealthy from a global perspective. Eventually, Europe rebuilt its industrial capacity. Japan started its long expansion to become the world's second-largest economy. A number of small export-oriented developing East Asian nations also started competing on the world stage. World trade increased sixfold between 1948 and 1973. Economists give the Bretton Woods monetary system a great deal of credit for growing international commerce.

Yet the carefully constructed international monetary system fell apart in the early 1970s.[19] The system came under strain for many reasons, among them inflation and the oil price shock of the early 1970s. Money escaped from the regulatory boundaries that policy makers tried to impose. Speculators constantly sought out the highest returns possible. Multinational corporations expanded their operations worldwide.

The dollar was the reserve currency for most international transactions. Yet the world ended up with far too many dollars, the so-called dollar overhang. More than half of all international money transactions were financed with dollars, plus America had to fund enormous defense and foreign aid obligations overseas. Problem is, the dollar's value fell as inflation took off, with the government pursuing a policy of guns and butter during the Vietnam War. The dollar weakness shook the foundations of the post–World War II system. Gold flowed out of the United States, and everyone in international finance knew that America could not meet its promise to convert dollars into gold if asked. A series of compromises and agreements papered over the growing cracks in the system. However, the Nixon White House opted for severing the link between the dollar and gold in 1971. It was part of a series of drastic actions taken by Nixon and Treasury Secretary John Connolly to get the president reelected in 1972. Nixon won in a landslide.

Still, it's less important why Bretton Woods fell apart than its impact. Within a few short years, having gold or some other commodity not backing the currencies of major economic powers was no longer a temporary policy—a momentary suspension instituted during war or some other national trauma. The value of the dollar now relied on the commitment of the federal government to keep it stable. In essence, the U.S. government told the world: Take our word that a dollar is a dollar. Or, to be more accurate, have faith that the Federal Reserve is a stable anchor for the dollar's purchasing power.

As far as the dollar goes, the promise wasn't worth much more than the paper it was printed on, at least at first. The Fed gradually learned through trial and error what it took to ensure the dollar's value in a fiat currency world. Milton Friedman was right: the Fed printed way too much money in the '60s and '70s. Investors, workers, managers, entrepreneurs, policy makers, homemakers, and consumers came to expect that prices would always be higher next month and next year. The Fed essentially believed that a little inflation was tolerable so long as a fast-growing economy created jobs and kept unemployment down. Indeed, many economists and policy makers believed they could drive the unemployment rate down as far as they wanted so long as they were willing to live with a higher inflation rate. In other words, there was a trade-off between unemployment and inflation, and the haunting memories of the 1930s made the policy decision easy.

The Fed was far from alone in welcoming inflation. So did equity investors scarred by deflation during the Great Depression. Indeed, the most popular explanation for stock market appreciation in the early 1960s was inflation. Sidney Homer was a pioneering bond market researcher at the Wall Street trading firm Salomon Brothers. Inflation is the enemy of fixed-income investors, since higher prices erode the value of principal and interest payments. In the 1960s, Homer gave a series of fascinating talks before equity investors. He emphasized how much the stock investor hailed inflation. Homer pointed out that thousands of market newsletters, economic papers, finance articles, and brochures proclaimed, "Inflation, as everybody knows, is good for the stock market." Wall Street reporters commonly attributed a gain in the Dow Jones Industrial Average to evidence of renewed inflation, he said. But Homer strongly disagreed with the idea that inflation was to be hailed. "It is my intention today to question this truism of finance," said Homer in an address before the Security Analysts of San Francisco in 1967. "In fact, over the years a minority of voices have been heard to protest that inflation is not good for stocks. . . . Nevertheless, it is still a heresy."[20] Imagine saying that today.

America was also engaged in the Cold War with the Soviet Union and other communist nations. The global battle was partly ideological, and it was important for politicians to show workers that welfare capitalism was superior to communism. So, if inflation accompanied fast growth, well, maybe that wasn't so bad.

The Triumph of the Financiers

But the sense grew that inflation was spiraling out of control. Prices kept going higher at the pump, in the supermarket, and at the car dealer. Carter was no Nixon willing to sacrifice the economy for reelection. Miller was shuttled off to the Treasury, and Paul Volcker, the extremely independent president of the Federal Reserve Bank of New York, became Fed chairman. Volcker was determined to crush deeply ingrained expectations of ever higher prices among consumers, business, investors, and the international community. So was his successor, Alan Greenspan. Changes in monetary policy affect the price level with a long and variable lag. It took a long time for the Fed to establish its inflation-fighting credentials.

Volcker and Greenspan succeeded because they were determined to use the power of the central bank to defeat inflation. The economic and political climate had also changed. No one was worried about deflation anymore, not in an environment where getting inflation down to 10% was considered success. Inflation was the economic problem to confront. A large body of economic research, much of it done by such notables as Milton Friedman, Edward Prescott, Robert Barro, Robert Lucas Jr., and Edmund Phelps, upended many economic policy assumptions. For instance, the trade-off between inflation and unemployment turned out to be false. Over the long run an expansionary monetary policy leads to higher inflation without lowering unemployment. Many popular culprits behind the inflation spiral, such as wage demands and higher oil prices, didn't pan out, either. No, it was up to the Fed to take the inflation-fighting lead. Indeed, that was the message the financial markets sent to the Fed—remain steadfast against inflation or watch interest rates climb ever higher, strangling growth, and increasing ranks of the unemployed. The bond market vigilantes never let the Fed change course. The Fed, along with central banks around the world, came to the conclusion that the best monetary policy was one that solely or almost exclusively focused on price stability. That, and to act as lender of last resort during financial crises, such as during the 1987 stock market crash or in the immediate aftermath of 9/11.

Inflation accelerated the dismantling of managed capitalism. The changes are largely associated with the rise of the right, particularly the election of Margaret Thatcher of Britain in 1979 and Ronald Reagan as U.S. president in 1980. Thatcher, Reagan, and their followers openly embraced conservative economists like Milton Friedman and Friedrich Hayek and more popular polemicists such as George Gilder and Arthur Laffer. But democrat Jimmy Carter embraced airline deregulation and appointed the hard-nosed Paul Volcker as head of the Fed. The turn toward markets didn't only sweep America and Britain but also Chile, Eastern Europe, the Soviet Union, and even China. Many liberal economists and policy makers that had little use for Hayek or Laffer, let alone Reagan and Thatcher, were also enthused about the embrace of the market including deregulation, stable money, free trade, and unleashed financial markets. "So the shorthand we came to deploy among ourselves was to speak of 'the Market Revolution,'" says David Warsh, a longtime economic journalist.[21] Whatever the transformation is called, it was a critical step toward the Age of Deflation.

A striking moment was May Day, 1975. That's when Wall Street deregulated commissions. Wall Street had long preached the benefits of competition for everyone but brokers and investment bankers. But financiers found it increasingly untenable to not allow customers to shop for cheap commissions. The Securities and Exchange Commission was going to force the industry to change, so the New York Stock Exchange deregulated commissions. Fees plummeted, a number of firms failed or were taken over, and the stage was set for the rise of the discount broker and eventually online trading. Interest rate caps in the financial services industry were removed, and competition among banks, thrifts, brokers, insurance companies, securities dealers, and so on was encouraged. The antitrust law was relaxed, contributing to a wave of mergers and acquisitions. Many trade barriers were dismantled.

The explosive growth in the global capital markets is critical to the end of inflation. In recent decades, financiers in industrial nations have poured trillions into building satellite and fiber-optic communications networks that span the globe. Walter Wriston, the former chairman of Citicorp and a leading architect of modern electronic finance, once declared, "Information about money has become almost as important as money itself." The rise of the global capital markets lowered the cost of saving and borrowing; the pool of investment capital soared as more people gained access to the markets; financial innovators exploited new opportunities to create products and markets, which in turn further lowered the cost of capital; and so on in a dynamic dialectic. This money wasn't controlled by governments, or even elites in business and finance. Millions and millions of savers around the world put their savings at risk in the capital markets. If the Fed, or any central bank, seemed willing to debauch the currency, money fled with the click of a mouse.

Going Forward

Remember when Wall Street considered Federal Reserve Board Chairman Alan Greenspan the most powerful man in the world, a master of the universe? Money managers dismissed any worries about the stock market with reverent quips like, "In Greenspan we trust." During Senator John McCain's 1999 campaign for the Republican nomination for president, he memorably captured Greenspan mania. "I would do like they did in the movie *Weekend at Bernie's:* I would prop him up, put a pair of dark glasses on him, and keep him for as long as we could," McCain said at the time.

Ah, how the mighty have fallen. Following the bear market in stocks and the downturn in the economy, people stopped raising their glasses in praise of Greenspan. And a growing number of his economic peers criticized him for not bursting the stock market bubble toward the end of the 1990s. Reputation is a tricky commodity. When times were good, Greenspan could do no wrong, although Wall Street greatly exaggerated his power to steer the world's largest economy during tranquil years—let alone when economic storms struck. No person or institution is omniscient enough or has the tools to keep the economy on an even keel.

Still, the dissing of Greenspan misses the point. Greenspan's great achievement is (1) establishing the Fed's credibility as a force against inflation, turning the dollar into a brand-name currency, and (2) realizing that with inflation down it was time to listen more to the market. Like Andrew Carnegie, George Eastman, Sam Walton, Robert Noyce, or other towering entrepreneurs in American business history, Greenspan saw better than his peers that new information technologies would create a productivity revolution. "One could write volumes about changes in business from Carnegie to Noyce," writes Harvard Business School professor Richard S. Tedlow in his book *Giants of Enterprise: Seven Business Innovators and the Empires They Built.* "One point, however, stands out when we discuss the titans who mastered change. . . . [They] either created new technology or welcomed it. All of them exploited it more skillfully than the competition."[22] Greenspan is an economic entrepreneur who exploited the edge between ideas and policy by recognizing that so long as the Fed stayed the course, inflation wasn't going to emerge in the Information Age. Thanks in large part to technological innovation, international competition, and the rise of market forces around the globe, the Fed's job became easier. It was a virtuous cycle.

Many reform proposals for maintaining price stability are gaining a serious hearing these days. A number of academic economists argue the Fed should establish strict inflation targets, like Canada and New Zealand. Others, including Fed chairman Alan Greenspan, argue that it's better for everyone to understand the goal is price stability, but a bit of leeway should be left. What's striking is how uniform the trend is toward low inflation to no inflation to deflation no matter whether there is an explicit target or not. The upshot: the battle for price stability is never-ending. John Maynard Keynes called inflation and deflation "evils to be shunned." It is still true. This is a new world where the prospect of deflation has to be taken seriously.

CHAPTER 9

BUSINESS AND WORKERS IN AN ERA OF FIERCE PRICE COMPETITION

> The circumstances of the ever-changing
> market and ever-changing product are
> capable of breaking any business organization
> if that organization is unprepared for
> change.
>
> —ALFRED P. SLOAN JR.

DEFLATION ISN'T ABOUT TO GO AWAY. THE FED and the global capital markets will adhere to a goal of no inflation, which in reality translates into strong deflationary pressures in a hypercompetitive high-tech global economy. The trend toward a stable to falling price level is a cause and a consequence of radical economic and technological changes that are creating enormous bounty and dislocation in the American economy.

Now, outside the plunge in the price level, the most striking economic statistic during this era has been the dramatic increase in productivity growth in the past decade, and, as we've seen, higher productivity is a factor behind inflation's demise. Productivity, or the amount of output per unit of input, has been growing at more than a 3% average annual rate since 1995, significantly better than the 1.4% yearly pace of 1973 to 1995. And small differences in the productivity numbers add up to big changes over time. Living standards double every 28 years at a 2.5% long-run trend of productivity growth; and 35 years at a 2% pace.

Living standards tend to soar in an economy with high productivity and stable to falling prices. But the good news doesn't wash with a lot of people. Companies routinely downsize, slashing and burning their payrolls. Many individual investors are still scared by the losses they suffered during the long bear market of 2000 to 2003. Millions and millions of poorly educated workers are stuck in menial, low-paying jobs with slim prospects of entering the middle class. Well-educated middle-class employees and technological wizards are fearful of losing jobs to cheaper peers in India, China, the Philippines, and elsewhere in the developing world. Job insecurity is rampant—and with good reason. The gap in perception between how economists view the world and the average employee is apparent whenever I participate in a call-in show at Minnesota Public Radio on the state of the economy, or take questions after a speech at a public radio event in major urban areas around the country.

Some of the pessimism may be sour grapes, a perspective infected in part by an overly romantic vision of how well our parents had it coupled with a too dour take on present circumstances. The astute social commentator Greg Easterbrook, in his book *The Progress Paradox*, carefully documents just how much better off most Americans are materially than their parents and grandparents, not to mention the immigrants who entered the country through Ellis Island.[1] Easterbrook notes that in 1956 the typical American had to work 16 weeks for each 100 square feet of home purchased; it now takes 14 weeks of work, and the amenities are a lot nicer. American children and teenagers usually have their own bedroom, an unheard-of luxury for previous generations. Americans take vacations around the world, and purchase for a reasonable price gadgets that until recently only the rich could afford. We're advancing like gangbusters on many social issues, too: the workforce has never been so highly educated. Americans are living longer, healthier lives. Crime is down. The environment is cleaner. To be sure, inequality has widened, but if you take out the impact of immigrants, the gap narrows for the remaining 89% of the population, partly driven by rising incomes among African-Americans. And immigrants bring so many benefits to the United States that the concern over rising inequality is misplaced. As 19th-century historian Edward Gibbon noted, "There exists in human nature a strong propensity to depreciate the advantages, and to magnify the evils, of the present times."[2]

But the disquiet is too pervasive to ignore. The horror of September 11, war in Afghanistan and Iraq, and an uneasy realization of how vulnerable America is to another terrorist attack are gnawing worries. At an even deeper level, however, Americans were telling pollsters even in the boom years of the 1990s that the country was "going downhill" and that their children "face a declining future." The percentage of Americans who describe themselves as "happy" to pollsters has not budged in half a century. The incidence of depression rose tenfold in the post–World War II period. One reason may be the age-old proposition that widespread material abundance cannot overcome a sense that our lives lack purpose. "A fundamental reason that acquiring money does not sync with acquiring happiness might be stated in cool economic terms," writes Easterbrook. "Most of what people really want in life—love, friendship, respect, family, standing, fun—is not priced and does not pass through the market. If something isn't priced you can't buy it, so possessing money may not help much."[3]

The popular gloom also stems from deflationary forces unleashed within the market economy. In a series of lectures, Richard Layard, director of the Centre for Economic Performance at the London School of Economics, summarized seven factors that recent social science research says affect happiness: income, work, private life, community, health, freedom, and philosophy of life. The scholarly work emphasizes the big negative impact that unemployment and job insecurity have on people's sense of well-being and contentment. The financial and psychic impact of getting laid off is enormous.[4]

Just ask David Hill, formerly an executive at the Internet company Trilogy in Austin, Texas. When the boom went bust, he was laid off a few weeks after his daughter's birth. The search for a new job took months, and in the meantime the bills mounted. "Let's say you've got $28,000 in credit-card debt. Okay. Your wife may have to work, but she doesn't know yet. You're trying to find work, and you don't know where you're going to end up yet, because this is a national search that's going on," said David. "You've got to figure out—can I sell my house? I might not even be able to sell my house for six months. Do I want to carry two mortgages? Are we going to rent? Where are we going to live? Are we going to buy where we're going to live? And how much can we afford there?"[5]

That's a strain on anyone. If unemployment is such a disaster, "it is also not surprising that, even when people are in work, they are much happier if they feel their job is secure," says Layard. Well, job insecurity will be endemic in a deflationary environment.

Corporate Pricing Power Is Gone

Management likes nothing more than to take out the markup pen and hike prices. Ah, when prices are soaring, increasing revenues and reported profits are as simple as changing a price tag. Sure, managers will complain about inflation, but pay raises are easy to justify when prices are rising, and take-home bonuses are generous. Inflation masks a lot of corporate sins. In sharp contrast, deflation is a stern taskmaster. Take this calculation from consultants McKinsey & Co.: a 1% drop in price will slash operating profits by more than 12% for the average Standard & Poor's 1,000 company, assuming costs and volume remain the same. Little wonder the pressure to cut costs and hike efficiency is relentless.

Smokestack America has been coping with falling prices since the early 1980s. Old-line industries were battered by the galewinds of international competition, government deregulation, and the takeover attacks of sharp-eyed corporate raiders. Falling prices are also a way of life in the high-tech business. It's an industry accustomed to growth as expensive gee-whiz technological breakthroughs become tomorrow's big-volume, low-price sellers. The price tag for supercomputers, personal computers, network servers, semiconductors, cell phones, personal digital assistants, Wi-Fi, digital cameras, and other high-tech gear have come down year after year even as power and function expand exponentially. Just ask Andy Grove of Intel, Steven Jobs of Apple, and Michael Dell of Dell Inc.

Dell, perhaps the world's most efficient company, became the world's leading PC maker with a pioneering build-to-order system designed around the Internet. Now Dell is pushing the efficiency frontier even further by automating more of its e-commerce network with assembly-line robots that process orders from the Web. The automated assembly line pumps out 900 computers an hour compared to 300 before. It's an intense focus on making more with less that allows Dell to keep slashing prices and grab more market share, while driving marginal players away from the business.[6]

What's striking now is how the price competition is spreading to previously immune sectors of the economy such as services and even the professions. The pricing pressure is forcing banks, transportation, insurance, telecommunications, retailing, brokerage houses, and other service-sector industries to emulate manufacturers to hike efficiency by investing huge sums in new technologies and reorganizing the workplace.

For example, during the long expansion of the 1990s, the major airlines kept their business fares high. An executive making a trip from Los Angeles to New York might pay over $1,200 while the person sitting next to her forked out $300 to visit family and friends.

The price gap allowed aggressive discount airlines like JetBlue Airways and Southwest Airlines to double their share of the market since 1995 to 20%. Today, bleeding red ink, the industry goliaths are fighting back, wringing wage and work rule concessions, slashing payrolls, and launching their own low-cost subsidiaries. Merrill Lynch, Morgan Stanley, and other brand-name brokerage houses charged small investors steep trading fees well into the early 1990s. Then online upstarts, like Ameritrade and E-Trade, came along offering individual investors razor-thin commissions. Merrill Lynch vice chairman Lincoln Steffens said that the "do-it-yourself model of investing, centered on Internet trading, should be regarded as a serious threat to Americans' financial lives."[7] He should have said a threat to the high fees pocketed by Merrill's brokers. Merrill eventually allowed its customers to trade online.

Remember when auto dealers charged customers the manufacturer's suggested retail price for a new car? For many of us, purchasing a new car was a miserable experience with knowledgeable, slick salespeople and wary, uninformed customers. There was an information asymmetry that favored the car dealer. No more. Internet companies like Edmunds.com and Cars.com opened up a wealth of car-buying information, including the car dealer's invoice price and discounts from the manufacturer. It's easy for customers to get a good deal today.

The Internet has transformed other service industries. A radiologist in India may read mammograms from New York. An accountant or financial analyst could be based in Malaysia. Electronic Data Systems, the Plano, Texas, computer services company founded by Ross Perot, is hiring Indians, Malaysians, and other educated workers elsewhere in the developing world. They maintain and update old software codes and manage computerized records for 401(k) benefits. In addition, U.S.-certified CPAs prepare corporate tax returns and offer back-office support for the company's consultants.[8] Companies are outsourcing some basic legal work to Mexico, Canada, India, and South Africa, according to Hildebrandt International, a New York–based legal consultancy.[9]

Even the pharmaceutical industry may be no longer immune to pricing pressure. The drug industry's highly profitable business model has long relied on charging Americans the highest prices in the world. But that may soon change. Several years ago, senior citizens living along the Canadian border started boarding buses to buy Prozac, Vioxx, Zoloft, Lipitor, and other prescription drugs that go for as much as 75% less in Canada than in America. This activity served as a catalyst for seniors across the country to turn to mail-order shops and online companies for cheap prescriptions, mostly from Canada. As this book is being written, the federal government and the drug industry are mounting a fierce defense against the reimportation of drugs. Legislative battles may be won, but it's a losing war—the pressure from customers to lower prices is proving irresistible. The same story is unfolding in the music business. The Internet is reducing the ability of sellers to price discriminate by charging a higher price to one set of domestic or international customers.

Indeed, the only industries with prices that seem to be headed higher over the long haul—in other words, not simply reflecting a surge in demand and a lack of supply—are those that have the help of government regulation. One example is cable television. Cable TV companies are often granted local monopolies, and the federal government has decided to keep out of regulating prices. The General Accounting Office, an investigative arm of Congress, documents that the average monthly rate for expanded basic cable service is $36.47. That is a price increase of 40% from 1997 to 2003, well above the rise in the CPI.[10] Satellite competition just hasn't been pervasive enough in most markets to make much of a difference. The two big exceptions to the trend toward lower prices, of course, are health care and education—two giant low-productivity service industries that have resisted the pressure to restructure.

Nevertheless, the direction of the price level includes all sectors of the economy, and the dominant trend has been down, gathering momentum and scope, for more than two decades. *Business Week,* the *Wall Street Journal,* the *New York Times,* and other major news publications have chronicled the impact of ever-lower prices on businesses, workers, and consumers. Beleaguered, frustrated managers looking for guidance have turned business books into bestsellers, such as *Who Says Elephants Can't Dance?* by Louis V. Gerstner Jr., *Execution* by Larry Bossidy, *Jack* by Jack Welch, *Only the Paranoid Survive* by Andrew Grove, and *The Innovator's Dilemma* by Clayton Christensen. What's different today is a matter of degree, of evolution, a realization that the pricing pressure not only won't let up but is spreading. Deflation is no longer confined to the economy's tributaries but has gone mainstream.

Of course, new information technologies are helping some companies price smarter. Databases and computer networks allow management to move away from traditional average cost and average pricing techniques. Companies can use information technologies to target customers who may be relatively indifferent to an increase and those extremely sensitive to higher prices. Similarly, the new information technologies let these companies better track customer preferences and keep tighter control over their prices.

The bottom line: managers and workers have had no choice but to rethink virtually every aspect of how they do business.

The Kinetic Corporation

In the past, internal processes determined price. Today, management is learning the opposite is the new norm—price determines process.

In the traditional pricing approach, a company comes up with a selling price by adding up its costs, factoring in overruns, and putting an acceptable profit margin on top. These days, such cost-driven pricing is a recipe for unacceptably high prices and a nice wide opening for lower-cost rivals. The plain reality is that customers don't care about their suppliers' costs. "One of the misconceptions about pricing is that it's a decision that can be made after everything else has been done to develop the product," says Jagmohan Raju, professor of marketing at the Wharton School. "But, actually, pricing needs to be an integral part of the plan for taking a product to market from the very beginning. It cannot be an ad hoc approach."[11]

Cost cutting in this environment, of course, is essential. But savvier managers have learned not just to whip out the markdown pen or simply lay off workers. To preserve profits and eke out growth, companies have been forced to come up with radically different corporate strategies, manufacturing techniques, marketing tactics, compensation structures, and financing approaches. Companies have redesigned products for ease and speed of manufacture or stripped away costly features that customers don't value. They're seeking to gain a bit of shelter from relentless pricing pressure by forging closer links with their customers or by accelerating new product development. They're burning the midnight oil figuring ways to improve productivity by tearing down bureaucratic walls and investing in high-tech hardware. "You have to be more productive and get costs out that aren't contributing to that productivity," says Robert Schnorbus, chief economist for JD Power and Associates, a Westlake, California, consumer marketing research consulting firm.

In 2003 Deloitte & Touche, the multinational consulting firm, surveyed 660 global manufacturing companies. Manufacturers that embrace quality management techniques, invest in equipment and organization, and work closely with customers enjoy decent profit margins even while cutting prices. Gary Carrington, Deloitte's director of automotive industry practice and national director of lean enterprise strategy, authored the study.

> The traditional approach says that the system is the solution. The emerging value that we see is that simplification is the solution. The old way of looking at quality was to inspect quality into the product. The emerging value is that quality should be at the source—

making or doing it right the first time. Another traditional value might define efficiency as working hard and working faster. The emerging value is that efficiency is effectiveness or, put another way, getting more with less. The traditional value as relates to employee management was "telling" staff how to do their jobs while the emerging value is to establish continuous learning and improvement. Where the traditional value was risk aversion, the emerging value is evolving into experimentation.

Investing in information technology for growth and efficiency is a necessary but not sufficient condition for productivity growth. Research by MIT's Brynjolfsson and colleagues found that for every $1 invested in information technology, there is another $9 of investment in work training, organizational changes, new business processes, and other "intangible" investments to get a decent return on investment. "For example, even with advanced data-analysis tools, no top manager can take full advantage of all the information available to a company. In fact, the problem of information overload and the resulting bottleneck of human information-processing capacity tends to worsen at the higher levels of the corporate hierarchy," says Brynjolfsson. "As a result, the most productive IT users were more likely to find ways to empower line workers and salespeople, and otherwise decentralize decisions."[12]

Take a Johnson & Johnson factory that makes adhesive bandages. It dramatically increased the variety of products it could produce at a cheaper cost after combining new computer-based flexible machinery with a dozen carefully defined work practices and principles, according to the study into productivity by Brynjolfsson and his coauthors, Lorin Hitt of the University of Pennsylvania and Shinkyu Yang of New York University. "The right combination of work practices was discovered only after a lengthy and costly period of experimentation and false starts," they write.

As in any dramatic conversion, many companies are stumbling as they grope for a more flexible, responsive corporation. Reengineering and restructuring are often management-speak for massive layoffs without any transformation of work or a shattering of bureaucracy. Surveys by consultants and academics show many companies cut too deep into their workforces and refuse to sufficiently delegate authority. Management's pursuit of higher productivity can mean demanding that people work longer hours, closing up a store on their own time, booting up their laptop on the weekends, or even "volunteering" at company-sponsored charitable events, all without compensation or reward. (Although senior management makes sure they get awarded gargantuan pay packages and lush retirement benefits to boot.)

Nevertheless, the signs point toward more and more companies trying to change. In the mid-1990s, I toured the Pitney Bowes plant in Stamford, Connecticut. Pitney Bowes is the world's largest maker of postage meters and mailing equipment, and my guide was Kevin Connolly, director of systems-products manufacturing. The company had collaborated with a local community college to devise a customized seven-stage training curriculum for its workers. In a manufacturing setting where more than 17 languages were spoken, five years before I walked around the plant about 40% of its 1,500 production workers were not literate to a fourth-grade level, and 65% required some kind of math training. Employees spent several hours a week in training sessions developing skills. The training had paid off, with almost everyone meeting the basic literacy and math requirements. Employees now worked in teams, collaborated with engineers, ordered materials, and monitored product quality. "These workers have homes and they make decisions all the time," said Connolly. "Yet in the past, we treated them as if they were incapable of making decisions when they came into the factory. No more."

A Case Study

Americans love their wheels. Most of us get to work, the grocery store, and the kids' soccer games in our cars. A car tells the world we're brash and fun-loving, hardworking and bold, or conservative and frugal. Other than a house, a car is perhaps the one way that Americans express who they think they are. Over the years, they've overpaid dearly at times to maintain and foster that image. However, that's not the case for many models now. Car pricing has been flat-to-down for years, especially after adjusting for quality improvements. For one thing, customers have had enough of sticker shock and many are no longer willing to risk their creditworthiness for a set of fancy wheels. Even more important, the competition for sales is vicious with Japanese, German, South Korean, and other overseas car manufacturers crowding into the American market.

One way automakers are keeping prices under control is by squeezing their suppliers. For more than a decade, car makers have been demanding annual price cuts of 3% to 5% for everything from bumpers to windows. Domestic automotive suppliers know that business as usual means going out of business, especially since overseas challengers control about half of the North American market. Yet whether domestic or foreign, somehow suppliers need to make the brakes, mirrors, drive trains, and other parts ordered by the major automobile companies at a cheaper price—and still turn a profit.

What are companies doing? The response has been dramatic. They're speeding up the development cycle, which in turn requires stitching together teams from engineering, design, finance, marketing, and production. It means empowering workers and using lean manufacturing techniques. It means working closely with suppliers to deliver quality parts and collaborating with customers to generate savings. It means coming up with innovative products again and again. The payoff? High-performing auto supply companies have profit margins of 10.5% compared to an industry average of 5.1%. "Looking back, it was a tough 10 years," says Timothy M. Manganello, chairman and chief executive officer of Borg-Warner, a $3 billion revenue auto supplier. "The secret is this: If you have the leading technology, people will buy your product." Adds Kevin J. Adler, president and chief operating officer of Akebono Corp, North America, a Japanese-owned supplier based in Farmington Hills, Michigan: "We have strong cost-reduction activities. Those cost reductions focus on productivity improvement, commonization and standardization globally, new and evolving technologies and product development, and raw materials."

Gentex is a case in point. The Zeeland, Michigan–based company makes self-dimming mirrors. Maryann Keller, president of Maryann Keller and Associates, is a widely admired industry analyst who sat on the company's board. She notes that in the late 1980s the reject rate for mirrors was something around 20 out of every 100. Today the reject rate is around zero. Gentex's manufacturing productivity soared as it automated production and adopted lean manufacturing techniques. Its mirrors are now more than reflecting glass, since they now include map lights, compasses, outside temperature indicators, speakers, and so on. Thus, the dollar amount spent per mirror is going up even though the base price per mirror is decreasing, from around $100 in the late 1980s to about $15 today. "It has cut prices every year, as prescribed by the car companies, yet it has managed to expand profits and revenues," says Keller. "That's an example of a company that's been able to fulfill the expectations of the auto companies and been able to maintain a very high level of growth and return on assets."

It's hard for automotive suppliers to invest in worker training with profit margins so thin. But unless they do, profits could evaporate. Indeed, auto suppliers now train their workers on average about 40 to 50 hours a year per employee. That's an increase of almost 100% from a decade ago. For instance, at Borg-Warner, employees are involved from the earliest days of design through the manufacturing process, an unheard-of practice at the company 10 years ago. "It leads to better quality and better launches," says Timothy Manganello, CEO of Borg-Warner. He estimates the shift in employee involvement has improved efficiency 300% to 500%. "Concerning training, we do a lot of training. We train internally using our own people. We may also hire outside consultants. In some of our plants we've teamed up with local colleges," he adds.

Educated workers are more productive employees. Another way to improve efficiency and lower costs is to outsource production to cheaper regions of the world. For instance, the consulting firm Deloitte found less than 5% of the 70 automobile suppliers it surveyed were outsourcing to China five years ago. That figure has swelled to over 22%. Indeed, a major difference between a profitable auto supplier and a struggling one is how well the company manages its information and supply chain, especially through the Internet. Says David Littmann, chief economist at Comerica Bank, "It's a matter of survival. If you're not allowed to go outside the boundaries of your state or country to pick up your best labor costs, quality and speed from gestation of product ideas to production, you're history." Adds Professor Sawhney of Northwestern University's Kellogg School of Management: "The Internet enables offshoring and offshoring results in deflation."

Yet, the automotive industry has learned that there are limits to outsourcing, says Dr. Sean McAlinden, chief economist and director of the Economics and Business Group at the Center for Automotive Research at the University of Michigan. Automotive technology is patent-protected—a concept suppliers are finding may not be respected in some emerging economies, notably China. The quality of components made offshore is not always as good as it should be. Some components, such as heating and air-conditioning systems, power seat components, and exhaust systems, are too fragile and expensive to be built abroad and shipped back to America. Considerations of just-in-time inventory management and currency exposure, as well as the importance of staying close to customers, also put a brake on too much outsourcing. Put it this way: It's a global economy. Even as U.S. manufacturers expand their business overseas, Toyota, Nissan, Honda, Mercedes, and Hyundai are expanding their presence in America.

Fact is, American companies are globally competitive because of the openness of the U.S. economy. Business here has lived longer than its overseas adversaries with red-hot competition. With the world's largest consumer market luring foreign rivals, battles for markets and profits are relentless. With a government eager to deregulate, market forces have been unleashed in everything from telecommunications to financial services. With a society open to entrepreneurs, upstarts have shaken up industry after industry.

At the 2003 management briefing seminars, an annual industry self-examination attended by key decision makers of automotive manufacturers and suppliers worldwide and sponsored by the University of Michigan Center for Automotive Research, Alfred H. "Pete" Peterson, chief executive of Peterson Spring with 900 employees, gave a nod to overseas challengers that have about half the North American market. "They got it by providing good product for good value. They have also introduced some new DNA into our automotive industry gene pool. Toyota's TSSC, Toyota Supplier Support Center, for example, teaches the Toyota Production System to members of the traditional North American supplier community." Peterson called for established U.S. companies to emulate the maniacal focus on employee involvement, customer collaboration, and constant quality improvements and cost reduction throughout the total supply chain.

The Pressure Cooker Economy

As we've seen, price pressure and restructuring aren't confined to manufacturing. The details might defer, but in essence service and information companies are increasingly copying the same playbook: investing in high-tech gear, reorganizing the workplace, slashing costs, hiring educated workers, outsourcing, rewarding innovation and creativity, and boosting productivity, all with an eye to increasing profits. Restructuring, reengineering, and downsizing—pick your favorite buzzword—will remain a permanent part of management's tool kit in any industry.

Contrary to conventional opinion, restructuring often doesn't mean a smaller workforce at a company. What is more common is shedding workers in a profitless division and adding workers to operations with growth prospects, or getting rid of one type of employee in order to make room for others with a different set of skills. For instance, of the group of companies that announced a downsizing program that made the pages of the *New York Times* and the *Wall Street Journal* between 1993 and 1997, half of the firms several years later had a labor force at least as large as when the planned layoffs were announced. A majority had increased their workforce by a hefty 10%, according to economists William Baumol, Alan Blinder, and Edward Wolff. Creative destruction is a tough environment for workers, with lots of employment and lots of churn.[13]

There is also pressure to keep wage costs down. That's why so many companies are trying to change wage and benefit formulas from a fixed cost to a variable plan through merit pay, profit sharing, bonuses, stock options, and other techniques more directly tied to a company's fortunes. So, instead of committing to a fixed salary of, say, $40 an hour, companies will offer workers $30 an hour, plus the chance to take home merit, bonus, and profit-sharing payments. In good years workers can earn more than the $40 they would get under the traditional pay system, but in bad years their pay package will be slimmer. "The more costs are variable, the more companies can stand cyclical swings," says Nick Galambos, vice president at the international consulting firm A. T. Kearney. "If more of your costs are variable, you're not going to be as advantaged on the upside, but you're also not going to be as disadvantaged on the downside."

Economic flexibility is the other side of the job insecurity coin. The economy is increasingly able to weather severe shocks. For instance, a quarter of all employees now keep schedules with varying work hours and work times, up from one-sixth a decade ago. Some three-quarters of all companies use performance bonuses, about one-half offer profit sharing, and over one-third provide stock options. "Labor, capital, and product markets are increasingly adept at adjusting to shifts in demand, technology, and the various shocks emanating from the global economy," says Mark Zandi, chief economist at Economy.com.

CHAPTER 10

WHAT KIND OF RETURN
CAN INVESTORS EXPECT?

Tis the part of a wise man to keep himself
today for tomorrow, and not venture all his
eggs in one basket.

—DON QUIXOTE DE LA MANCHA

MAIN STREET IS NOW WALL STREET. INDEED, THE
swift reaction by regulators and industry to the
Great Mutual Fund Scandal of 2003 and 2004
shows how much the small investor is the real
power on Wall Street. Investing has all the char-
acteristics of a mass social movement, like home
ownership following World War II or credit cards in the 1960s.
With more than half of U.S. households owning stocks and over 95
million Americans parking their savings in mutual funds, the average person now has a direct stake in the performance of the capital
markets. The trend will only strengthen as the baby-boom generation, now in its peak savings years, gets ever closer to retirement.
Like so much in American society, investing has gone mass market
and middle class.

To be sure, individuals flocked to the stock market in the late
1920s. But after the crash of 1929, individual investors spurned
stocks for the next three decades. America's newly prosperous mid-

dle class did return to wagering on stocks during the Go-Go Years of the 1960s and the Nifty Fifty craze of the early 1970s. Yet the cult of mutual fund performance spectacularly flamed out, and prices of big-capitalization growth stocks cratered. Disgusted with Wall Street, net annual outflows from equity mutual funds in the 1970s ranged between 1.2% and 11.9%. That compares to a brief outflow of less than 1% from equity mutual funds in 2002, and investors were net buyers of stock mutual funds in 2003.

So, why have individual investors in the aggregate largely stuck with stocks this time? It all reminds me of the Sherlock Holmes dialogue about the dog that didn't bark.[1]

> "Is there any point to which you would wish to draw my attention?"
> "To the curious incident of the dog in the night-time."
> "The dog did nothing in the night-time."
> "That was the curious incident," remarked Sherlock Holmes.

The curious incident in the stock market is what didn't happen: individual investors didn't flee the market in a panic, despite the searing economic and business trauma of the past three years. Think about it: America lived through the bursting of the dot.com bubble, the tragic attacks of September 11, and wars in Afghanistan and Iraq. A recession and feeble recovery. A three-year bear market. Business scandals. A depression scare. Federal budget deficits as far as the eye could see. Now, if somehow you had known back in 2000 that this was the future, wouldn't you have forecast the biggest stock market collapse in Wall Street history and a mass exodus by individual investors?

One reason for the lack of panic is that individual investors may be more diversified than common lore holds. Everyone knows someone or has read about investors that suffered an 80% or 90%

loss on their portfolio, usually by putting all their eggs in one basket—high-tech stocks. Sad to say, some of these unwitting gamblers have had to postpone retirement or go back to work. Still, the tales may be misleading in the aggregate. For instance, the Employee Benefits Research Institute/Investment Company Institute database covers 16 million active plan participants in 49,000 401(k) plans holding $619 billion in assets. Taken altogether, 40% of the retirement money was invested in equity mutual funds, 9% in balanced funds, 33% in fixed-income securities, and 16% in company stock. The youngest workers had more of their retirement money saved in equities—64%—while the oldest workers had the least—43%. These are reasonable asset allocations and indicate that the bulk of workers with access to a retirement-savings plan are behaving rationally with their long-term investing. Even more important, Americans have no choice but to turn to the financial markets to fund their retirement, their children's college education, and other long-term aspirations.

The transformation of savings is in part a result of the corporate campaign to rein in costs. In short, the 401(k). Companies retreated from offering their workers expensive traditional "defined benefit" pension plans in favor of low-cost "defined contribution" plans such as 401(k)s, 403(b)s, and the like. With the traditional defined benefit pension plan, the employer bears all the investment risk and commits to a fixed payout of money, typically based on a salary and years-of-service formula. In sharp contrast with the 401(k) and similar tax-deferred retirement savings schemes, workers take greater responsibility for their retirement plans and funding arrangements. Employees decide how much money to invest and where to invest it, depending on the limits established by law and the choices offered by the employer. Employees bear all the investment risk.

Thus, most Americans today have a direct stake in how deflation will affect stock and bond market values over the long haul. The mass movement toward putting long-term savings into the stocks and fixed-income securities means that the market's fortune during deflationary times isn't an intellectual curiosity, or only a concern of elites. It may well be the difference between eating caviar or fish eggs during retirement.

It's a scary, unsettling change that only adds to worker insecurity. Sure, the trade-off of less financial security for the opportunity to earn greater wealth seemed reasonable during the great bull market of the 1990s. The risk inherent in investing became all too apparent during the 2000–03 bear market, however. Nevertheless, Main Street has no choice but to put money at risk in the capital markets. "By necessity, not by preference, people are becoming more involved in creating their own security by doing their own homework and making their own decisions," observed Charles S. Sanford Jr. in a talk given while he headed up Bankers Trust in 1993. "This pervasive sense of vulnerability is putting risk management at the top of the agenda for many people and organizations."[2]

Forty-something Pat and Terri McKeown are typical. Pat is a director of information systems for a publishing company in Minneapolis, and his wife, Terri, is a freelance graphic artist. Pat's dad retired from the railroad, and he has a regular monthly income coming from retirement, but Pat knows he'll never get that kind of pension fund. Instead, he participates in his company's 401(k). Both he and Terri are troubled by the financial risks they are taking. "It seems like a big gamble to me to be in the stock market watching everything that's going on and how quickly things change," says Terri. "I have to admit I don't have a great understanding of the financial world."[3]

The Pats and Terris of the world have no choice but to educate themselves better about the markets. The good news is that history suggests they'll make a decent return off the savings they put into the market during deflation. History may not repeat itself, as Mark Twain said, but it rhymes.

The Markets During the Great Depression

Now, mention deflation and the markets, and most people will recall the stock market crash of 1929. Stocks had been lurching lower after reaching a peak in September, and on October 29 the Dow plunged by 30%. Volume reached a record 16.4 million shares, an infamous benchmark that held for 40 years. From its 1929 peak of 381.17, the Dow Jones Industrial Average plunged to 41.22 in July 1932. At the end of the decade, equity investors had earned a mere real 1.43% from 1929 to 1939. It wasn't until 1954 that the benchmark index passed the level it had reached before the 1929 crash.[4]

Like the 1990s, the stock market seemed everywhere during the go-go years of the 1920s. Yet despite the colorful tales of cab drivers, bootblacks, clerks, housewives, doctors, lawyers, and other ordinary folk gambling their life savings in the stock market, historians now believe that no more than 8% of the population owned stocks, and most of those investors were well heeled. Wealthy or not, many investors lost fortunes. Comedian and singer Eddie Cantor supposedly lost 2 million dollars. Songwriter Irving Berlin didn't heed the advice of Charlie Chaplin to get out and lost a bundle.[5] Irving Fisher, widely ranked among America's greatest economists, damaged his reputation by loftily predicting shortly before the 1929 crash that stock prices had reached "a permanently high plateau." Worse, a large part of his wealth disappeared in the crash.

Obviously, stocks did horribly during the Great Depression. But bonds did well. Interest rates and bond prices are two ends of a seesaw. When bond yields are rising (usually from investors anticipating higher inflation), bond prices go down, and vice versa. Bond prices soared as bond yields came down sharply during the Depression. For instance, the prime corporate bond yield average went from 4.59% in September 1929 to 3.99% in May 1931. Investors earned a return of 6.04% on their money during the 1930s. Short-term fixed-income securities or bills returned 2.65% over the same time period.[6] But even fixed-income investors are wary of deflation, since unwary creditors absorbed huge losses during the 1930s as cash-strapped corporations and beleaguered municipal governments defaulted on their debts.

Two Wall Street tycoons who ended up with pockets full of money after the crash were Alfred Lee Loomis and his partner and brother-in-law, Landon Thorne. The two had been leading financiers for the new electric power industry in the 1920s. Loomis was also a scientist, and he became a major supporter of some of the century's greatest scientific minds at his Tuxedo Park home. By early 1929, the two partners had liquidated all their stock holdings and put the gains into long-term Treasury bonds and cash. The reaction by their peers, so many of them forced out of business, seemed more like envy than admiration, since "in the midst of so much despair, with the economic situation deteriorating day after day, Loomis and Thorne continued to profit handsomely," writes Jennet Conant, author of the Loomis biography: *Tuxedo Park: A Wall Street Tycoon and the Secret Palace of Science That Changed the Course of World War II.*[7]

Mild Deflation and the Markets

The overall price level fell at a frightening rate during the Great Depression. The investment record is different when deflation is mild, however. In many cases, deflation and hefty investment returns in both stocks and bonds have coexisted. Indeed, history suggests that the stock and bond markets thrive so long as deflation is relatively modest.

Let's look at some numbers, courtesy of Steven Leuthold, a Wall Street investor and market historian. The stock market rose on average 14.6% during the 24 years of mild deflation (the CPI flat to down 2.4%) from 1872 on. That's second only to the 15.3% average gain in an environment of slight inflation (growth in the CPI hovering between 0.1% and 2.0%). However, after adjusting for the price level, periods of mild deflation jump to the top of the stock market performance sweepstakes. Stocks earned a real average annual return of 15.8% during mild deflation versus a real 14% gain with slight inflation.[8] Bonds did well, too, during mild deflations. No matter how you slice the data, the message remains the same, says James W. Paulson, chief investment officer at Norwest Investment Management. "Stock and bond returns run neck-and-neck when inflation is not a worry."

There is a rub. If mild deflation turned into a severe downturn, defined as the CPI falling 2.5% or more, stocks did abysmally. (Stocks also put on a comparably poor performance during extreme inflation.) "The major determinant of stock market performance is whether or not deflation is mild (controlled) or strong (uncontrolled)," according to the Leuthold Group, a stock market research firm.

A Look Ahead

Well, what sort of return can investors expect going forward? Now, the essence of investing is uncertainty, especially with the economy making a transition from inflation prone to deflation prone. You can't eliminate the uncertainty. As Peter Bernstein, the dean of finance economists emphasizes, it's in the nature of the beast. When Albert Einstein died, he met three Americans outside the Pearly Gates. To while away the time, he turned to the first American and asked, "What's your IQ?" The man replied, "190." "Good," said Einstein. "We can discuss the general theory of relativity."

Einstein then turned to the second American. "What's your IQ?" he asked? "150," the man replied. "Wonderful, we can talk about prospects for nuclear disarmament," said Einstein. Feeling quite cheery, Einstein turned to the third man. Again, he asked for his IQ. The man hesitated and finally muttered something that sounded like "80." Einstein paused, looked at the man, then said, "What's your forecast for the markets?"

Surprise is endemic in the markets. In the 1950s, Wall Street was stuck in the doldrums even as the U.S. economy stirred and American business dominated world markets in auto, steel, and other mass production businesses. Memories of the 1929 stock market crash lingered with the public, and professional investors constantly fretted about "another '29." Stock dividends yielded some 7%, but the wealthy sought safety in bonds paying 3%, while the middle class preferred putting their money into banks and thrifts offering depositors some 1.5%. It was not obvious at the time, observes University of Chicago finance professor John Cochrane, that the United States would enjoy half a century of growth never before experienced in human history.[9]

Averages can be misleading too. Take the well-known figure that the stock market has returned an average annual gain of almost 11% since 1926. The problem is, on average Lake Erie never freezes, and more than $8.5 trillion dollars in stock market wealth didn't vaporize during the last bear market. The trajectory of stock and bond market returns is far more complicated than pictured by a casual glance at a chart displaying annual gains recorded over decades. A closer reading of history books and contemporary accounts shows investors struggling to cope with cataclysms such as World War I, World War II, and September 11; mass enthusiasms for radical new technologies like railroads, radio, and the Internet; and political shocks ranging from trade disputes to protest movements. Take the decade 1869 to 1879. Equities returned a real 10.10%, bonds 8.49%, and bills 8.79%.[10] The decade included the "Black Friday" panic of 1869, the "Crime of '73," the Black Hills gold rush, the invention of the mimeograph machine, telephone, phonograph, and incandescent lightbulb, a railroad boom and bust, the massive railroad strike of 1877, the Crédit Mobilier scandal that disgraced the Grant administration, an international debt crisis, the retreat from Reconstruction, and so on. Hardly tranquil years.

Those caveats are important to keep in mind in all seasons. The accounting for the market's performance following the end of great bull runs is also sobering. It took about two decades for investors to recover their enthusiasm for equities after the peak of 1901. Stocks returned −0.2% from 1901 to 1921, after adjusting for inflation. The Kennedy-Johnson bull market peaked in early 1966, with the Dow Jones Industrial Average hovering around 1,000. Seventeen years later, the world's most famous market benchmark was still struggling to break 1,000. Taking into account the high inflation of that era, the Dow declined some 60%.[11] That said, there are good reasons to believe that individual investors will earn decent returns on their stock and bond investments. For one thing, financial securities do well during mild deflations. For another, the productivity promise of the new economy suggests the economy can grow at a rapid pace. One line of forecasting is to tie stock market returns to the economy's performance. In the long run, stock returns reflect corporate earnings growth, which in turn is closely linked to the economy's growth rate. Many economists now believe the U.S. economy can grow at a 3.5% to 4% average annual rate without generating any inflationary pressures. Add to that a dividend yield—about 1.6% in 2003—and a real return between 5% and 6% is a sensible probability. That's in line with the stock market long-term inflation adjusted return of 7%. If there is a surprise, it could be on the upside, if growth in the new economy is stronger than expected.

A return of 5% to 6% doesn't sound like much, but only against the benchmark of the dazzling 12% average annual return on stocks from 1982 to 2001, after adjusting for inflation. Much of that return represented a historic transition from high interest rates and high inflation to low interest rates and no inflation, as well as the collapse of communism.

The bond market's salad days are over, too. Bonds performed phenomenally well as interest rates plunged from double-digit to low single-digit levels over the past two decades. Mathematics alone suggests that with bond yields at 40-year lows, there is little capital appreciation left in fixed-income securities. The return on bonds is primarily determined by the interest rate, so a return somewhere between 3% and 4% is realistic.

Stocks should outperform bonds, although by a small margin. The equity risk premium for much of the post–World War II era has been huge, with stocks outperforming bonds by 7 percentage points from 1946 to 2003. Modern finance theory says stocks should outperform bonds because equities are riskier, representing the uncertain earnings returns to entrepreneurship. Stocks are more than twice as volatile as bonds. (The annualized volatility of stocks is about 20% versus 8% for bonds and 1% for cash.) Stocks are also riskier than bonds because when a company encounters financial trouble, bond holders have first dibs on corporate cash flows while equity holders carry the brunt of any losses.

Economists have written thousands of papers debating why the postwar equity risk premium was so huge. But there seems to be an agreement that the risk premium will be narrow going forward. The main reason is that over the past two centuries the equity premium has largely widened or narrowed depending on the bond market's fortunes. Bonds do well when lenders are confident their money is safe from the ravages of inflation. For instance, the equity premium was 1.9% a year from 1816 to 1870 and 2.8% annually from 1871 to 1925. A study by Robert D. Arnott and Peter L. Bernstein argued that the risk premium rarely hit 5% over the past 200 years, with the exceptions of war, its aftermath, and the Great Depression. Instead, the historic average risk premium is a modest 2.4%.[12]

This overall forecast dominated by macroeconomic trends and corporate dividend policy doesn't rule out heady periodic bursts of investor enthusiasm, largely around new technologies and markets, followed by a bust—what Princeton University finance economist Burton Malkiel calls "occasional trips to the looney bin."[13] Investors are prone to bouts of enthusiasm and depression, to overestimate and underestimate risks, to follow the crowd into the latest hot investment and to rush for the exits along with everyone else. As a matter of course, prices stray from fundamental value, and no one is ever really sure whether a stock or the stock market is undervalued or overvalued. The late Fisher Black, one of the so-called rocket scientists at Goldman Sachs best known for his work on pricing options, once defined a well-working market as one in which price is within a factor of two of value. So let's say the market puts a value of $100 on a company or an index. Let's also assume that the fundamental value of the company or index is $100 a share. Even then, given all the uncertainty surrounding corporate earnings, new product development, economic activity, and competitive threats, investors could reasonably price the company or index as high as $200 and as low as $50, according to Black's theory. "The factor of two is arbitrary, of course," wrote Black. "Intuitively, it seems reasonable to me, in light of sources of uncertainty about value and the strength of the forces tending to cause price to return to value."[14]

That seems reasonable to me, too.

Investing for All Markets

Whenever I am on the road, I spend part of the morning flicking between the various business and finance television programs. The only chance I ever get to catch these shows is when I'm traveling. The business and finance programs have many strengths: solid information, plenty of market and economic numbers, an increasingly international perspective, and some decent interviews with chief executive officers, high-level government officials, and other well-placed elites. Still, these shows are also troubling because of their incessant hyperventilating over the latest rumors, market gossip, and fast-buck trading schemes, along with an obsession with finding the next winning stock. It's as if everyone watching were a Wall Street trader wannabe and an aspiring hedge fund gunslinger. Well, most of us aren't. Fact is, the television shows highlight a great divide in the world of investing: the entrepreneur and the insurance buyer. And knowing which you are can save you from a lot of money mistakes.

Entrepreneurs, whether they call Wall Street, Main Street, or dot.com home, are out to make big bucks. And they're willing to risk losing a bundle, perhaps everything, in their pursuit of a large payoff. Entrepreneurs are obsessed with their business. It's what they do and what they are. Entrepreneurs are constantly seeking an information edge on the competition, and they spend a lot of time learning about their business. Many of these risk takers use leverage—lots of borrowed money—to magnify their potential gains and losses.

Now, contrast that approach with your neighbors and your peers at work who are investing in the stock market. I bet most of them—including you?—are periodically setting aside some earnings for the stock market through a retirement savings plan, a 401(k), or an IRA. They may be putting additional savings into an equity mutual fund or a state-sponsored 529 college savings plan, to help pay for their children's college education. In essence, what they're doing is taking out an insurance policy against the risk of a lower living standard in retirement or to limiting how much their children will have to borrow to attend college. The goal is to constrain the downside rather than to reach for untold riches.

Which would you rather be called, an entrepreneur or an insurance buyer? Most of us would pick entrepreneur. Yet "insurance buyers" investing in the stock and bond markets will do well financially over the long haul and still have the time to do many other things that matter.

Trying to beat the market is a loser's game: Thanks to hordes of investors, equity researchers, mutual fund money managers, journalists, day traders, hedge fund operators, corporate treasurers, pension fund managers, and all the other players investigating stocks, struggling to decide whether stocks are overpriced or underpriced, equity prices often reflect much that is known about a company. Phenomenal sums change hands every day, as millions and millions of very smart people (and many more not-so-smart ones) try to get an edge on the competition. What often moves stock prices is new information, which by definition is unpredictable. Terrance Odean and Brad Barber, two finance economists at the University of California, Davis, looked at the trading accounts of more than 66,000 households at a large discount brokerage firm from 1991 to 1996. The stock market recorded an annual return of 17.9% during that period, while those who traded the most, after taking into account commissions, scored just 11.4%. Now you know why they named their paper "Trading Is Hazardous to Your Wealth."[15] Individual investors who trade stocks by the hour or the week, or those who move in and out of mutual funds several times a month or quarter, are wasting time and money. No evidence shows that all that trading activity creates wealth. Abundant data show that a disciplined, long-term approach with minimal trading increases the odds that you will reach your long-run financial goals.

What matters is managing risk: the only way investors create the opportunity to earn a higher return is to take on greater risk. Risk means different things to different people, and that should be reflected in investment portfolios. It's not just an appetite or distaste for embracing uncertain outcomes. A tenured professor enjoys a level of job security that allows for greater risk taking with investments, assuming a bold temperament. A marketing account executive on commission is always at risk of losing her job, and a more conservative portfolio is usually sensible. Rather than worry over whether now is the time to buy into high-tech stocks or flee bonds, investors should spend some time mulling their comfort level with regard to financial risk.

Diversification pays: Despite the hours most individuals spend pouring over stock tables and mutual fund rankings, most finance economists agree that how investors allocate their assets is the primary determinant of their long-term performance. The essential insight behind asset allocation is that different investments carry distinct risks and rewards. To get the most out of investments, investors should focus on their ability to withstand financial risk and their time horizon, then come up with an investment mix that closely mirrors both. "The reality is with an asset allocation approach you will never do as well as the best-performing class or as poorly as the worst-performing asset class," says Ross Levin, a certified financial planner and president of Accredited Investors Inc. "But you will do well over time."

A related concept is diversification, the notion of not putting all investment eggs in one basket. Everyone got a lesson in the benefits of diversification over the past three years. For instance, the Russell 3000 returned −4.18% and the Russell 200 growth index −7.61% on an annualized basis in the 4 years ending in December 2003. The Vestek Broad bond market index returned 9.21% and the Vestek 90-day T-bill index 3.44% over the same time period. The trick is to mix and match the major market assets to create a well-diversified portfolio for good times and bad.

For many people, diversification includes putting some money into foreign markets. The idea of investing overseas to cushion swings in the U.S. market has fallen into disfavor in recent years. The world used to be made up of national markets, and the relationship or correlation between countries was relatively weak. Investors could both reduce the risk of their portfolios and enhance returns through geographic asset allocation. But with goods, services, capital, and labor crossing the globe as never before, the correlation between the U.S. stock market and foreign bourses has tightened considerably. There's no question that seemingly local events can reverberate throughout the world economy with greater force than before. That's one theme of this book. But economies and markets are far from marching in lockstep. Overseas diversification still works as a risk-reduction strategy. To be sure, there are lots of risks associated with going overseas. Countries can devalue their currencies or clamp on capital controls. Accounting standards are weak and economic information poor. Political instability is a fact of life. Emerging markets are extremely volatile. Nevertheless, for long-term investors the strategy that seems to make the most sense in a global economy is a global one.

Index. Index. Index. Actively managed mutual funds take too much of an investor's hard-earned savings. Taking into account high turnover costs, sales charges, and other expenses, they average close to 3% a year. John Bogle, the founder of the giant mutual fund company Vanguard and an industry gadfly, estimates that during the 1984–2002 period the average mutual fund returned slightly over 9%, versus a 12% annual return for the S&P 500.[16] The fees on broad-based equity index funds hover around 0.20%. What's more, most professional mutual fund money managers aren't worth their huge salaries, since the pros fail to beat the market with any consistency. The benchmark S&P 500 stock index outperformed 84% of actively managed large-capitalization equity funds over the last 10 years and 88% over the last 20 years, according to finance professor Burton Malkiel. Broad-based equity index mutual funds are the way to go for most individuals. So are exchange traded funds (ETFs), index funds that trade on the major stock exchanges. Index funds are simple. Fees are razor thin. Trading costs are minimal.

Money isn't the only cost when it comes to actively managed funds. Time is another. You have to ferret out good mutual fund money managers, then monitor them closely. That's tough to do. Sure, we'd all like to find the next Warren Buffett or George Soros, but how do we find them with any assurance when the new phenoms are in their early 20s and not basking in their achievements in their 70s? Warren Buffett, the legendary stock picker, is a strong advocate of careful research. But if knowledgeably poring over balance sheets and studying management is not your passion, he recommends index funds. "By periodically investing in an index fund, for example, the know-nothing investor can actually outperform most investment professionals," Buffett wrote in 1993. "Paradoxically, when 'dumb' money acknowledges its limitations, it ceases to be dumb."[17]

Fixed-Income Securities

With inflation dormant and prices flat to down, fixed-income investors should enjoy decent returns. And it may sound strange in a book arguing that the dominant price trend is deflation, yet most long-term investors might want to consider putting most of the bond portion of their diversified portfolio into Treasury inflation-indexed securities—generally known as TIPS. For one thing, inflation-indexed securities preserve the purchasing power of money. For another, they are a hedge against the risk of needing to cash in some fixed-income investments when inflation is spiking higher. Many individual investors will find it cheaper and easier to purchase the Treasury's inflation-protected savings bond, the so-called I-bond.

Economists have long spoken in favor of bonds indexed to inflation. The federal government belatedly began issuing inflation-indexed bonds in 1997. Britain pioneered the modern market in 1981. Some 20 nations now sell these securities, usually benchmarked to a consumer price index. American investors have never truly embraced inflation-indexed securities. For one thing, the government started selling them at a time when investors were pocketing double-digit equity market returns. Who wanted to own a bond with a real return of 4.4% in January 2000, when the Nasdaq had soared by 65% and the Dow Jones Industrial Average was up 18% over the preceding 12 months? When the equity markets tanked, investors remained somewhat cool toward TIPS, with the Fed talking about an "unwelcome fall in inflation."

The reason to own TIPS and I-bonds isn't lush returns. TIPS and I-bonds are hedges against an untimely surge in inflation, say, around the time you're retiring or your kid is heading off to college. Unlike gold, the traditional haven against a debauched currency, owners earn interest from their bond investments instead of paying storage and other costs for a sterile asset. In the case of sustained deflation, the principal value of TIPS will decline. But should the principal value fall below 100 cents on the dollar, the Treasury is committed to make up the difference when the bond matures, because the maturity value of the bond never falls below par. The same goes for I-bonds. The bottom line: whether you're an inflation optimist, as I am, or a pessimist, TIPS and I-bonds are a savvy way to preserve the purchasing power of capital.

Both TIPS and I-bonds have two components to their interest rate: a fixed rate set for the life of the bond and a consumer price index semiannual inflation adjustment. There is a critical drawback for individual investors contemplating TIPS: taxes. In essence, you have to pay taxes on your inflation-adjusted gains before you ever get any of your inflation-adjusted money at maturity. That's why these bonds work best in a tax-deferred retirement savings account such as an individual retirement account or a 401(k) plan. That way, you won't have to worry about paying taxes until after you retire. The big attraction of I-bonds for individuals is that investment money compounds tax deferred until the bonds are cashed in. And like the mainstay Series EE savings bond, there are no commission costs for buying and selling I-bonds.

Home Isn't Just Shelter

Home sweet home may be a needlepoint cliché hanging on walls in many homes, but the phrase does capture a deeply felt sentiment in America. The housing market has been strong for years. It's not just the buying and selling of new and existing homes that sizzles. Walk the crowded aisles of Home Depot, Restoration Hardware, and Pottery Barn, and you'll see the boom in home improvement and remodeling at work.

The housing market will slow down largely because price

appreciation has run ahead of household income growth. The housing market frequently stalls, but prices rarely collapse like the Nasdaq in 2000 or oil prices in 1986. It's only when job losses skyrocket and personal incomes plunge that home prices spiral lower, as during the Great Depression or in the Southwest's oil belt during the 1980s energy bust. Far more typical is the supply of homes on the market drastically reduced when prices get too low. Many people just take down the "for sale" signs. That reduced supply helps prop up the market. However, in certain markets prices are so high today that the downturn will be brutal.

Still, the forces of supply and demand look healthy for the long haul. One reason is demographics. Household formation ran about an average of 1.25 million annually during the 1990s, and household growth likely will average 1.23 million a year over the coming decade. New households are being formed all the time. Newly married couples set up their own nest. A divorced partner searches for a new residence. The number of single women with good incomes and careers buying their own homes is skyrocketing. Immigrants are avid home buyers as their economic circumstances improve with time. Many see home ownership as a milestone toward assimilating into their adopted country. The aging population supports the housing market, too. Middle-age workers are in their prime earning years, and they're typically eager to own a place they can call their own.

What sort of return can investors expect? In a word, subdued. One potential measure of residential real estate's long-term return comes from a study by economist Karl Case of Wellesley College. He calculates that from 1850 to 1992, real estate's after-inflation return was 2.5% a year.[18] The data comes from 16,000 unencumbered land sales in Middlesex County, Massachusetts. Another, slightly lower figure comes from Mark M. Zandi, chief economist and a founder of Economy.com, an economic consulting firm. He expects a real return of some 1.5% a year over the next 20 years.

Investing in Human Capital

There is only so much money anyone can set aside year after year in savings. Perhaps no more than 10% in a world of single-digit returns. That's why many people will have to work well into their sixth decade. Indeed, retirement is increasingly looked at as a transition to another work life, although at a more relaxed pace. The Census Bureau reported in 2000 that 37% of men and 31% of women ages 55 to 64 were employed full- or part-time while receiving pension income. Those percentages are likely to go higher, since 8 in 10 baby boomers say they plan on working in retirement, according to AARP, the giant lobbyist for the over-50 crowd.

The social movement toward embracing work during the last third of life calls for a much broader definition of investing for retirement. The typical retirement worksheet deals with financial assets such as equities, bonds, cash, and real estate. But investing for the long term should also encompass education, training, and networking—what economists call human capital. Economists estimate that human capital in America is worth an estimated three to four times the value of all assets, including stocks, bonds, and housing.[19] "Investing in human capital is an investment like any other, and you can make it at any stage in life," says Zvi Bodie, professor of finance at Boston University.

Working longer can make a huge difference in retirement living standards. Pocketing even a slim income often allows retirement portfolios to compound over a longer period of time. For example, a $400,000 portfolio at age 55 compounding annually at a 5% rate with a $1,000 contribution a month is worth around $579,000 at age 60. But if earning an income means the portfolio is left alone to compound at a 5% rate over the next five years—even with no new contributions—it will grow to around $738,000.

More than making money, working is physically and mentally energizing. Take Carol Thompson. She had been a licensed clinical social worker with both a private practice and a job dealing with child custody cases for the superior courts in the San Francisco Bay area. Her work was rewarding but draining, and after some 40 years on the job she looked forward to leaving it all behind her. But then what? Although she took years to close down her consulting practice, she wanted something else to do. One day, while strolling through the University of California's Botanical Garden in Berkeley, she noticed a call for volunteers. She signed up but then soon started taking courses in horticulture at Oakland's Merritt Community College. Now, she's a highly knowledgeable, valued volunteer working with professional botanists in the plant propagation department. "There is something really stimulating but humbling about starting something new," says Thompson. "It's really an anti-Alzheimer thing to do."

CHAPTER 11

THE NEW REGIME AND PUBLIC POLICY

We must encourage capitalism, it being the
hope for the poor of the world and being in
any case what we are, but our capitalism need
not be hedonistic or monadic, and certainly
not unethical. An aristocratic, country-club
capitalism, well satisfied with itself, or a
peasant, grasping capitalism, hating itself,
are both lacking in virtues. And neither
works. They lead to monopoly and economic
failure, alienation, and revolution. We need
a capitalism that nurtures communities of
good townsfolk, in South Central L.A. as
much as in Iowa.

—DEIDRE N. MCCLOSKEY

THE TEMPTATION AT THIS STAGE OF A BOOK IS TO
write all the policy reform proposals that I
believe would make the world a better place. But
this book is about the technological and organizational transformation of the economy and society, and the promise of rapid economic growth
and higher living standards during a deflationary era.

Monetary policy is key. My assumption is that the Fed's commitment to price stability, reinforced by the global capital market's abhorrence of inflation, won't change—or maybe I should say can't change. The commitment to price stability lends a deflationary cast to the price level. That doesn't mean there won't be inflation scares. There will be. The Fed also reacted quickly to prevent a Japanese-style deflation from taking root in the United States in 2003. Yet the Fed, while it did a good job analyzing the prospect of deflation, was unusually unsure of itself when it came to responding to deflation. The Fed sent out mixed signals, confusing investors and business. Since deflation is not going to go away, the Fed should seriously consider how worried it should be about a falling price level. For instance, the "Friedman rule" developed by economist Milton Friedman three decades ago suggests that the optimal monetary policy requires "a rate of price deflation that makes the nominal rate of interest equal to zero," says V. V. Chari, economist at the University of Minnesota. In other words, the inflation rate should hover somewhere between −3% and zero.[1]

The odds are worrisome, however, that during the next downturn deflation could take a turn for the worse. Now, when the Fed governors fanned out across the country to reassure the public, they repeatedly mentioned that the central bank had a number of tools in its monetary toolbox. But most of these methods are untested. Meanwhile, the Fed needs to be constantly on the ready to confront the threat of a global financial collapse. Investors will flee any currency—including the American dollar—if the global capital markets decide the brand is being debauched through unsound fiscal and monetary policies.

Yet the Fed is an institution that has a single-minded mission: price stability. It will learn what it takes to run a sound money policy.

Embrace Free Trade for a Better World

Other public policies are a lot harder to achieve, and demand political will. Right now, many people hear a "giant sucking sound." That was 1992 presidential candidate Ross Perot's description of how America was losing jobs to Mexico. A decade later, it's not just Mexico that has people riled up. It's China, India, Taiwan, South Korea, Brazil, Chile, and other emerging markets. Workers are worried about losing their jobs, incomes, and benefits to overseas rivals. Industry after industry facing pressure to cut costs and lower prices is knocking on lawmakers' doors in Washington, blaming unfair competition.

Protectionism is a big mistake. Despite its negatives, the economic benefits of freer trade and open markets are simply too good to pass up for the developed and developing worlds alike. The economic evidence and history overwhelmingly support the view that freer trade invigorates economic growth by encouraging the spread of new commercial ideas, new technologies, and new ways of organizing everyday life.

Trade and innovation are accelerated with access to larger markets. For example, a computer program written in Washington State that could only be sold in Washington State is far less valuable than one that can be sold the world over. Put somewhat differently, Stanford University economist Paul Romer calculates that if a developing nation imposes a 10% across-the-board tariff, the cost in investment and profits from the new economic activity being blocked by tariffs could run as high as 20% of gross domestic product.[2]

Indeed, if there is one public course of action that most economists agree on, Republicans and Democrats, supply siders and Keynesians, Harvard economists and University of Chicago economists, it's the lush economic return from keeping borders open. "The judgment of economists," says Lawrence Summers, an economist and president of Harvard University, "the judgment of almost all of those who have thought carefully about the question, is that increased openness to trade makes a country significantly richer than it would otherwise be and makes its workers better off than they would otherwise be. And the primary reason why that is true is that they are able to import goods at lower cost and therefore their paychecks go further and their income, after correcting for the prices of things they buy, is substantially greater."[3]

The integration of the rich and poor nations of the world is not a zero-sum game where the gains of one come at the expense of the other. And driven by the rapid democratization of information, technology, and finance, globalization is turning out to be a remarkably progressive force. The Internet, for example, is a global communications network that is hostile to privileged elites and closed-minded bureaucracies.

The biggest problem in the world economy today is too little globalization. Far too many nations, including many of the world's poorest countries in Africa and the Middle East, are insufficiently tied into the global economy. That's why the rich nations should not only resist protectionism but also take bold steps toward strengthening the integrated world economy. President Clinton, in his last tour of Europe during the twilight of his presidency, spoke at Britain's Warwick University and called upon the world's wealthiest nations to let the poorest countries freely compete for markets where the latter have a natural advantage—like agriculture. "If the wealthiest countries ended our agricultural subsidies, leveling the playing field for the world's farmers, that alone would increase the income of developing countries by $20 billion a year," Clinton said. The International Food Policy Research Institute calculates that eliminating trade barriers to food would generate an economic benefit of nearly $36 billion for both the developed and developing regions of the world by 2020.[4]

What's more, farm subsidies have largely failed as public policy. More than steelworkers, miners, or high-tech innovators, family farmers represent America's ideals of Jeffersonian democracy, close-knit community, and attachment to the land. The "family farm" exerts a powerful pull on the American imagination even in a nation that is largely urban and suburban. "They are images that hearken back to when life was simpler," says Karl Stauber, head of the Northwest Area Foundation. "Part of it is I think the romantic notion that we have about other people having a simpler life where good and evil are much clearer. You're out there doing God's work—converting raw land into productivity."

Some of the nation's most disturbing and stirring images come from family farmers combating weather catastrophes and economic calamities, such as the Joad family and their neighbors in John Steinbeck's *Grapes of Wrath*. Steinbeck captured the tragedy of farmers dispossessed by big farms and big banks during the Great Depression. "They come with the cats . . . the cats, the caterpillar tractors. And for every one of 'em, there was ten, fifteen families thrown right out of their homes. A hundred folks and no place to live but on the road. . . . One right after the other, they got throw'd out. Half the folks you and me know throw'd right out into the road."

Farmers had been hit hard by plunging prices during the Depression, and it's stories like this that moved the government to start subsidizing agriculture in 1933 under FDR. The Agricultural Adjustment Act—a centerpiece of the New Deal—raised crop prices by paying farmers to cut back on production. Seven decades later, the government still heavily subsidizes the farm industry. Yet in 1935, there were nearly 7 million farms in the United States. Today there are only about 2 million. Farmers now make up less than 2% of the workforce, down from 21% in the early 1930s. Over the past two decades, farmers have received more than $300 billion in taxpayer-financed support, and the subsidies aren't working. "I understand the political and romantic base for encouraging people to stay in farming, but I would argue we are better off helping those people to make the transition to other kinds of enterprises, to other kinds of opportunities," says Stauber. "Right now, I would say much of our federal policy and much of our state policy is sending the message stay in it, it will get better. Well, it's gotten marginally worse every decade for the last four to five decades."

The case for free trade has never been easy. Many economists are adherents of the doctrine, ever since Adam Smith extolled the international division of labor (efficiency and productivity gains from access to bigger markets) and James Mill articulated the principles of comparative advantage (countries produce what they do best and trade the finished products). Baby boomers have a selfish but vital stake in a healthy global economy. Some economists and investment professionals fret that when America's massive post–World War II generation retires and draws down their private pensions, the huge asset sale will depress stock and bond values, leaving boomers with low savings in their golden years. But the specter of a pension-asset implosion becomes less plausible the more that global capital markets grow. Here's just one measure: A decade ago there were perhaps 100 million equity owners worldwide, estimates David Hale, chief global economist at the Zurich Group. By 2010, he figures that the number could soar to 1 billion with the spread of pension funds throughout the developing world. Boomers will find plenty of willing equity buyers during their retirement years in a global economy. Otherwise, watch out.

Reform the Social Safety Net

That said, life is increasingly uncertain and insecure for workers. In an intensely competitive, fast-moving economy, many workers are losing jobs, forced to change careers, and must accept lower-paying jobs. Workers bear the brunt of capitalism's creative destruction. What should be done if the cost of protectionism is too high?

The most important reform is universal health care. The basic problem is that America's health care system for working-age families is employer based, and that system is both inefficient and inequitable. The fundamental flaw is that the company owns the plan, not the worker. Yet even though workers don't own the plan, they pay the full cost of the benefit through reduced wage increases. Worse, losing a job because a company's profits are down during a recession puts a family's coverage at risk. An employment-based system is guaranteed to increase the number of uninsured.

Look at it this way: Policy mavens at the conservative Heritage Foundation and the liberal Levy Institute rarely agree on anything. But both think tanks believe this is no way to run a health insurance system. "For me, as for many other economists, the connection between health care and a job makes little sense," says Walter M. Cadette of the Levy Institute. Adds Stuart Butler of the Heritage Foundation: "In our view, any attempt to deal with the problem that continues to subsidize employment-based insurance and merely adds new programs for families most disadvantaged by the current system, deals with the symptoms rather than the cause."

Coverage for health services started in the United States some 200 years ago with hospital care for sailors paid through compulsory wage deductions. Montgomery Ward purchased from London Guarantee & Accident Co. what's considered the nation's first group health insurance policy in 1910. Health plans expanded over the decades with Blue Cross & Blue Shield, HMOs, and group health coverage. Yet even by 1940 less than 10% of the population had some form of health insurance. The turning point was World War II. Wages were frozen but not employer contributions to health insurance. Companies bid for scarce labor by improving medical benefits for their employees. By 1950, half the population had some type of coverage—and today close to 60% of working families do. Health care benefits remain tax-free income to employees. Yet the United States never embraced universal coverage like Europe did following the Second World War, partly out of a historical distrust of big government and partly because powerful Southern political barons weren't about to vote for any system that extended health care to blacks.

There is no logic to maintaining today's badly frayed system.

Government should sever the link between coverage and the employer. One way to give ownership of health coverage to the consumer is by using a universal tax credit system paid in part by eliminating the tax exclusion on employment-based health benefits. Another approach that has been proposed by Victor R. Fuchs, the dean of health care economists, is a voucher given to all Americans financed by a broad-based tax earmarked for health care such as a value-added tax.

Both proposals carry a significant cost. But one of the biggest myths in public policy today is that we can't afford universal health insurance. The fact that the nation is projected to spend some 18% of gross domestic product (GDP) on health care in 2012, up from 15% currently and 7% in 1970, frightens a lot of people. Yet rising health care spending is not quite the devil it's often made out to be. The increased spending is improving quality of life—especially for older people—and generating a lot of economic growth to boot. And as medical advances open up new cures and the population ages, Americans may well want to spend more of their money on health care—not less. The higher a country's living standards, the more its citizens spend on their health.

For one thing, what we can afford depends on the rate of economic growth. Here's an illuminating calculation from economist Paul Romer of Stanford: The economy's underlying trend of growth from 1870 to 1992 was 1.8% (measured as income per capita). If that rate could be increased to 2.3% over the next half century, say through productivity improvements, the budget problems forecast for Social Security, Medicare, and Medicaid would disappear. Strong economic growth could resolve all the budget difficulties associated with the aging of the baby-boom generation, while leaving ample resources for dealing with any number of pressing health care problems.[5]

For another, many expensive medical treatments more than pay for themselves. That's what economists David Cutler of Harvard and Mark McClellan of Stanford found when they delved into the returns from medical technology used to treat a number of ill-nesses including heart attacks and cataracts. They found the net eco-nomic gain of treating heart attacks was some $60,000 per person.[6] Economist Frank Lichtenberg of Columbia University studied the returns on medical technology and medical care spending between 1960 and 1997. He calculated it cost $11,000 in medical spending and $1,345 in pharmaceutical research and development to gain one year of additional life. Meanwhile, the economic return for a year of life added up to $150,000.[7] Cataract surgery is now a half-hour out-patient procedure compared to hours in the operating room and days in a hospital bed in the 1960s. The inflation-adjusted cost of removing cataracts is the same today as in the 1960s, but many more people are getting treatment.

Of course, these numbers on the economic value of medical innovation only hint at the quality-of-life gains. Anyone who has had a low-birthweight infant, suffered from depression, or lived with impaired vision from cataracts knows what I'm talking about.

At the same time, medicine ranks high among America's most technologically innovative and globally competitive industries. The pharmaceutical companies and biotech outfits are systematically mining the genetic and research frontiers of medicine. Health is also a major employer. The Bureau of Labor Statistics reports that more than 9 million people—or 8% of the total workforce—work as health care practitioners, technical workers, and support staff.

The problem isn't devoting more of our economic wealth to health care. It's how we pay for our health care. When someone says we can't afford to keep spending more on our health, don't buy it. Lavishing more of our nation's wealth on health is a benefit we should all enjoy.

The other basic benefit crying for an overhaul is retirement savings. The current private retirement savings system is capricious. It includes 401(k)s, 403(b)s, 457s, SIMPLEs, SEP-IRAs, IRAs, and Roth IRAs, to name only the best-known plans. The rules, income limits, and restrictions vary significantly among most of these tax-advantaged savings programs. For instance, a 40-year-old worker at a company with a 401(k) can set aside a maximum of $12,000 in pretax dollars (in 2003), while an employee at a small company with a SIMPLE plan has an $8,000 limit. A stay-at-home spouse running the family household can save at most $3,000 in pretax dollars in an IRA. Worse, about half the population has no access to a private pension at work.

Again, why not attach the retirement savings plan to the individual and have just one rule for everyone—say, 15% of income, or $15,000. The figure could be less or more. The key point is that the rules should be uniform. The retirement plan should include "nonworking" spouses (an oxymoron if there ever was one). One way to achieve complete portability and the possibility of near universal coverage is to piggyback a voluntary program on the existing Social Security system. Workers could make additional contributions to Social Security, and the money could be invested in indexed stock and bond funds.

Last is developing a system of worker training and career shifts that better reflect the interests of employees, not companies. Right now, when the government moves to protect an industry from competition overseas, it puts up various trade barriers. Management continues to take down gargantuan pay packages. Consumers pay for the protection through higher prices. And protected companies continue to shed workers. A huge sum of money is wasted when it goes to protecting companies and their high-paid managements, although in the trolling for votes the high-visibility moves can pay off politically. It would be far more efficient for the federal government to subsidize laid-off workers with vouchers. The worker could use the vouchers at colleges, universities, community colleges, training programs, career counseling offices, and so forth. But it would be the worker who would decide what human capital investment makes the most sense for his or her circumstances. The federal government has made some steps toward a voucher training system. Still, protectionism carries more political appeal than vouchers targeted toward individuals. The

United States also spends far too little on training displaced workers. For instance, between 1985 and 2003, the Department of Labor funding for worker training declined by 29% when adjusted for inflation.[8] Yet the international competition for jobs and wages is heating up.

President Bush's "Ownership Society" approach is a step in the right direction. His goal is to simplify the confusing mass of government programs, allow individuals more control over their tax-deferred savings, and rely more on vouchers. But it can't be done on the cheap. The workforce needs more funding for training, especially as the demand for skilled workers grows and job churn accelerates.

Support Human Capital Investment

Wealth in the form that economists call "human capital" is worth three to four times the value of America's financial markets, housing, and other assets. Human capital consists of present and future earnings from investments in education, training, knowledge, skills, and health. And investments in human capital are vital in a shrinking, highly competitive world economy where companies can hire brainpower in the developing world over the Internet for a fraction of wages paid in the United States. Policy makers should focus their efforts on increasing the supply of talent that can transform ideas and information into high-tech products and marketable services. "The rapidity of innovation and the unpredictability of the directions it may take imply a need for considerable investment in human capital," said Federal Reserve Board chairman Alan Greenspan at a national governors' conference in State College, Pennsylvania, on July 11, 2000. "Even the most significant advances in information and computer technology will produce little additional economic value without human creativity and intellect."[9]

We've done it before. As the 20th century dawned, Britain,

Germany, America, and other industrial giants worried greatly about falling behind their major economic competitors. Businesses in every nation were concerned about a lack of skilled workers as a new high-tech economy emerged, marked by the spread of electrification, the internal combustion engine, and the embrace of scientific research by industry. Then the idea quickly took hold—the key to robust economic growth was people and training, not technology and capital. "Education might uplift, build moral fiber, enhance art, literature, and culture, and produce public officials, as even the ancients knew," says Claudia Goldin, an economist at Harvard University. "The novel concern at the dawn of the 20th century was that post-literacy training could make the ordinary office worker, bookkeeper, stenographer, retail clerk, machinist, mechanic, shop-floor worker, and farmer more productive, and that it could make a difference between an economic leader and a laggard," says Goldin.[10]

It took an enormous public investment, however, to turn this insight into reality. The United States led the way, largely through the expansion of secondary education. The record of the "high school movement" is remarkable. Goldin notes that in 1910 less than 10% of young people graduated from high school. Yet by 1940 the median 18-year-old in America was a high school graduate. In sharp contrast, European nations confined their secondary education efforts and expenditures to an elite cadre of youngsters. Goldin's research suggests two factors largely accounted for the revolutionary American approach. For one thing, in a dynamic economy with high rates of internal migration, the demand was for flexible, widely applicable skills that weren't tied to any particular place, industry, or occupation. The second major influence was an egalitarian tradition embraced by most parts of society since the early days of the republic. The push for mass education rather than elite education came from a widespread grassroots movement of local associations that wanted to keep their communities viable and democratic.

The good news is that most other nations are now emulating the American approach to mass education. Many of the world's wealthiest nations have caught up with—and some have surpassed—America in educating their young people. Even poor countries are investing heavily in secondary education, especially as their economies grow and incomes rise. For instance, school enrollment rates for girls are weak in the poorest countries—those defined as having a per-capita income below the American level in 1900. But when the per-capita income rises above that level in developing nations, gender distinctions all but disappear, with the exception of some Muslim nations. The payoff in these trends should be faster rates of economic growth in many developing nations—and in the world economy—in coming decades. America needs to expand its commitment to education to keep good jobs and incomes here.

Education reform is contentious. But American employers do value an educated workforce. Ideas and skills matter more than brawn and endurance. So, if conservatives are serious about equality of opportunity for all citizens, rather than stacking the game for the benefit of the few, public education should become an extremely well-funded crusade. And if liberals are earnest about attacking inequality, then they should realize that society's compelling interest in education and the interests of the education establishment aren't synonymous.

Let's start with early childhood education. The scheming laid bare by disgraced Wall Street analyst Jack Grubman's e-mail trail is a fascinating and appalling story. In brief, the $20 million–a–year telecom analyst for Citigroup's Salomon Smith Barney securities firm wanted his twins admitted to the 92nd Street Y nursery school, among Manhattan's most exclusive preschools. He successfully lobbied for the help of Sandy Weill, Citigroup's legendary chieftain. The philanthropic arm of the nation's largest financial services institution made a $1 million donation to the Y not long after Grubman's plea. Then Grubman abandoned his longstanding skepticism about AT&T's earnings prospects, a ratings upgrade that made it easier for Salomon Smith Barney to gain the telecom company's lucrative underwriting business. Everyone involved denies there were any quid pro quos involved, but no matter what, it sure looks like a sorry story of crony capitalism at work.

Of course, anyone who has lived in New York is hardly surprised. Ambitious Manhattanites will go to extraordinary lengths to get their children into the handful of prestigious private preschools widely seen as the first step toward an elite private school, then an Ivy League college. Still, this isn't an "only in Manhattan" story. It's more a perversion of a far less alarming phenomenon: well-heeled and well-educated parents everywhere are taking early childhood development seriously, spending enormous sums on educational toys, arts, crafts, and music, teaching babies to speak with signs, and, yes, in many cases investing in the "best" preschools. Sometimes parents lose a sense of proportion and balance. We're talking toddlers, after all. Yet the essential insight is right: the payoff from high-quality early childhood development programs is enormous.

Sad to say, studies suggest that as many as 40% of youngsters are entering kindergarten unprepared. Children from low-income households concentrated in the nation's major urban areas are especially at risk. Many of these youngsters never catch up during their elementary and secondary school years, eventually joining the ranks of poorly paid workers with few skills and even fewer prospects. "It won't matter if the economy grows 2% or 6% a year, this part of our society won't reach its potential if we don't give them the opportunity," says Arthur Rolnick, head of research at the Federal Reserve Bank of Minneapolis.

Many problems are intractable. Not this one. Government should provide disadvantaged youngsters with a high-quality preschool learning environment. Economic studies suggest that the return on investment in early childhood development is a huge 14% to 15%, after adjusting for inflation. To put that figure in perspective, the long-term real return on U.S. stocks is 7%. The gains from early childhood development programs include better performance in school, improved job and earnings prospects, and less risk of jail time. That's why resources and attention should be targeted to the kids who are most in danger of falling behind. The price tag is steep to provide a quality early education program for each low-income child, most likely twice the approximately $5,000 per child provided now by Head Start, the government-funded preschool program. But the public money is available. It's really a matter of funding priorities. Farmers will receive $182 billion in taxpayer subsidies over the next 10 years, even though the subsidy track record for farming over the past seven decades has been dismal. "Any company will invest in a high-return product, and so should government," says Rolnick.

Poorly performing elementary and secondary public schools, especially in the nation's major urban centers, are a concern. They leave too many minority children behind. They also handicap the achievements of those students who end up going to college. Some economists argue that at least part of the wage gap between college-educated whites and blacks reflects the odds that minority high school graduates attend colleges with less financial resources and lower average student achievement (measured by test scores) than the nation's elite universities.

What's needed is more choice and competition in public school systems, above all in inner cities. State governors and city mayors should outmaneuver teacher union activists and school officials to welcome Edison Schools, charter schools, and other independent operators with sophisticated management systems into their area. The federal government and state governments also need to pony up billions of dollars more for public education and target the funds at a region's weakest schools.

The college education system is in trouble. Support for higher education is the lever by which the government can move the entire economy. Yet state governments have been slashing their commitment in an era of tight budgets and rising medical costs. Three-quarters of college students attend public institutions, and those campuses make a sad picture. The decline in backing for public colleges by state legislatures and governors was exacerbated during the recent economic downturn, but it's an underlying trend. State budgetary obligations to pay for Medicaid are crowding out higher education. To take just one of many possible figures, state appropriations for higher education relative to personal income have fallen from roughly $8.50 per $1,000 in personal income in 1977 to $7 per 1,000 in 2003. State appropriations would have been about $14 billion higher if the ratio had stayed the same from 1977 to 2003.[11]

Scientific and technical knowledge is critical to economic growth, and much of that work comes out of universities. The government could create incentives to increase the amount of scientific education offered to undergraduates and graduates. Economist Paul Romer, a leading new growth theorist who works out of the Stanford Business School in the heart of Silicon Valley, has proposed that the government take active steps to boost the number of undergraduates majoring in science, mathematics, and engineering. The goal is not to create more academic Ph.D.s but to increase the brainpower moving into private-sector research and development. One idea Romer has put forward is for universities to compete for government grants based on their success in increasing the fraction of their students who receive undergraduate degrees in science, mathematics, and engineering. Another proposal is for the government to dramatically increase the number of "portable" fellowships that the government awards directly to scholars who show promise. Again, the idea is to direct funding toward the individual, who will then take his or her skills and initiative to the institution that offers the best prospects.[12]

Of course, overhauling the education system takes time. In the meantime, policy makers can dramatically increase the supply of skilled and educated workers by immediately boosting the immigration numbers of scientists, engineers, programmers, and others by the hundreds of thousands. Educated immigrants may be steroids for economic growth. American universities are very successful at attracting foreign students, and many of these foreign students stay here. By some estimates, a third of Silicon Valley workers are foreign born. What's more, immigrant workers create valuable trade bridges elsewhere in the global economy. The most striking recent example is the Indian diaspora that has done so well in Silicon Valley. Many wealthy Indian entrepreneurs are bringing home ideas, capital, and trade contracts.

There has been a move to make America less welcoming to foreign students and talented professionals. While the concern about security after 9/11 is genuine, the approach is mistaken. It hurts us economically as well as socially.

A focus on education will also address one of the more disturbing trends of the past quarter century: the rise in income inequality. The primary culprit has been technological upheaval. Employers put a premium on well-educated workers, expert at handling abstract concepts and comfortable with the new information technologies such as computers and the Internet. The notion that the new economy and the new inequality are synonymous is part of a very large literature. The benefits of a modern high-tech economy will only flow to a relatively small group of people. Everyone else will struggle to make ends meet.

Yet everything we know says that inequality shrinks with rapid economic growth. For instance, thanks to a 4% growth rate and a 4% unemployment rate during the 1995 to 2000 boom, companies snapped up minorities, women, seniors, and anyone else willing to work for a day's pay. The once unemployable found jobs and the working poor showed a big rise in their wages.

The inequality pessimists vastly underestimate the dynamism of the new economy and the ability of most people to participate in a high-tech economy—with a commitment to education. After all, the current association between economic inequality and technological breakthroughs is far from unique. Whenever major innovations take hold, income gains typically go to better-educated workers who can quickly master the new techniques and technologies. But history suggests that the payoff spreads as more people move up the learning curve and as additional innovations make the new technology easier to use.

Problem is, public policy optimism has been a scarce resource in recent years. The traditional animosities informing politics have worsened. The Bush administration genuflects to Ronald Reagan's legacy, but the dour, muscular crowd in the White House doesn't share Reagan's sunny "Morning in America" optimism. Democrats pay rhetorical tribute to Bill Clinton, but no one is willing to emulate his embrace of the New Economy. Both parties appeared to believe that the American economy is no longer an engine of growth. Politics is a battle over what both sides perceive as a zero-sum economy—one side could only gain at the other's expense. The only leading figure in Washington with unshaken faith in the economy's vigorous potential is septuagenarian Alan Greenspan. But his fervent belief that American enterprise is only starting to tap the productivity potential of the Information Age was increasingly dismissed as the tarnished perspective of an aging New Economy cheerleader.

Greenspan's right. And a commitment to education, as well as transforming the social safety net, will go a long way toward returning equality of opportunity as a major force in U.S. society. Of course, that means Washington needs to get its fiscal house in order.

Stabilize Fiscal Policy

"My name is Tom and I used to believe that fiscal policy was effective." Tom Stinson, a Minnesota state economist and an economics professor at the University of Minnesota, made that announcement at a policy analysis at the University of Minnesota in November 2002. "I have to confess [that] in the past six weeks or so, the environment in Congress has completely disabused me of a belief that fiscal policy could ever have an impact on the economic cycle. Almost every policy proposal is terrible," said Stinson.

To be fair, the Bush administration's massive tax cuts geared toward well-heeled citizens did eventually help resuscitate the economy. President Nixon once declared, "We're all Keynesians now." The British economist John Maynard Keynes was intimately associated with the idea that the federal government should spend more and tax less during a recession. The heyday of Keynesian fiscal activism came during the Kennedy–Johnson tax cut. The unemployment rate was 6.7% when President Kennedy came into office. The economy was sluggish, and many economists calculated that it was operating well under potential. Kennedy proposed a major tax cut in 1962, and President Johnson signed the measure into law in 1964. By the first quarter of 1966, more than seven million new jobs had been created, the unemployment rate had fallen from nearly 7% to less than 4%, and the nation's inflation-adjusted, after-tax per-capita income was one-fifth higher than in the first quarter of 1961.

Yet economists still debate whether the first deliberate attempt at Keynesian fiscal engineering really made much of a difference. Indeed, most economists have soured on the notion that fiscal activism could offset declines in private investment and activity in the short run. One major reason for fiscal skepticism is the realization that whatever Congress did to stabilize the economy was usually too little too late. By design, Congress is a fractious legislative body with genuine philosophical differences and competing constituent loyalties. Instead, economists saw the money mandarins at the Fed as better positioned to fight a recession. The Fed can turn on the proverbial dime, especially when compared to Congress. "I recall studies in the 1970s by Otto Eckstein and also by the Office of Management and Budget of the Carter administration that concluded that the timing of previous discretionary fiscal policies had actually been stabilizing," says Martin Feldstein, former head of the Council of Economic Advisors under President Reagan and a professor of economics at Harvard University.[13]

But this division of labor between Congress and the central bank only applies to short-run maneuvers for shoring up a weakening economy. Fiscal policy is crucial for promoting long-term economic growth.

The problem is, fiscal policy is a mess. Federal budget deficits as far as the eye can see are worrisome. It's not the actual dollar numbers that are scary. Supply siders are right. The U.S. economy is wealthy enough to easily carry federal budget deficits ranging from 4% to 6% of gross domestic product for years. There's nothing inherently wrong with a long-term federal budget deficit, either. Companies and households often run a deficit reflecting a rational decision to invest in future earnings—just ask a new homeowner. However, a corporate or household budget deficit can also signify confused priorities, a lack of discipline, and financial delusion, with catastrophic consequences—witness the travails of heavyweight boxer Mike Tyson.

No, it's the policy incoherence represented by the government's budget deficits that's disturbing. Fiscal policy is out of control. In the late 1960s and 1970s Democrat and Republican administrations pursued a policy of guns and social spending to minimize the economic pain of waging an unpopular war, and the budget deficit started its long climb higher. So did inflation. This time is different in one sense. The budget deficit is soaring as Washington pursues a policy of guns and tax cuts. The critical difference between now and the 1970s is that inflation won't take off. The Federal Reserve won't make the same mistake twice. The global bond market vigilantes won't tolerate it. The risk is not inflation but slow growth. The other danger of a profligate fiscal policy is that investors flee the dollar. The markets are jittery about Washington's spending binge, and the budget deficit could easily cause a crisis of confidence and a run on the dollar.

The White House and Congress should spend their legislative energies on simplifying a Byzantine tax code. Economists despair at the waste from the billions of hours and billions of dollars spent on administrative and compliance costs. Compliance costs associated with the federal income tax totaled some $195 billion in 2002, or a 20¢ compliance surcharge for every dollar taken in. Policy makers don't even try to defend a tax code that has ballooned from 26,300 pages in 1984 to 54,846 pages in 2003. Even tax professionals don't agree on the meaning of many rules. Just lower everyone's taxes as much as possible by eliminating most deductions, credits, and shelters. Stop favoring savings and investments, and treat investment income like all other income. For instance, the Bradley–Gephardt tax reform plan of the early 1980s had three brackets, with a top rate of 28% for individuals. The plan was constructed to keep tax reform from falling heavily on the poor and to preserve a few of the most popular deductions such as home mortgage interest and charitable contributions. I have no idea if the economy would grow faster with these changes. I believe it would, but I don't know for sure. What is certain is that such a system would be simpler, fairer, and easy to understand.

Another economic advantage from reforming the tax code would be fiscal stability. Milton Friedman has argued that lurches in the tax code have become a random disturbance to the economy, disrupting investment and other financial plans.[14] Think of all the economic uncertainty caused by tax law changes during the Reagan, Bush, Clinton, and Bush years. Why not embrace a progressive, lower-rate income tax system with fewer tax deductions but keep the most justifiable deductions like charitable contributions and home mortgages? It would be far superior to and much simpler than the current practice. "There is a lot of room for streamlining, simplification, and rationalization," says Joel B. Slemrod, an economist at the University of Michigan.

Supply-Side Economics

The real gains in the economy will come from the supply side. Public policy should boost the supply of knowledge, information, labor, and capital. Ever since Robert Malthus, the first economist, economics has been about scarcity, savings, and other puritanical notions. Yet how much material wealth has grown and how much scarcity has been relaxed although not banished since the Industrial Revolution is stunning. Given time, in the high-tech global economy, the bounty that was once largely confined to the modern industrial nations should be shared by the entire world—bringing everyone on the planet hope for a better life.

Notes

CHAPTER 1: "AN UNWELCOME SUBSTANTIAL FALL IN INFLATION"

1. "Greenspan: Not Enough Inflation," CBSnews.com, May 21, 2003.
2. *The Return of Depression Economics,* by Paul Krugman, W.W. Norton, 1999; and *Deflation,* by A. Gary Shilling, Lakeview Publishing Company, 1998.
3. "An Historic Moment," by Stephen Roach, Global Economic Forum, Morgan Stanley, June 23, 2003.
4. "The Fed: Wary, Weary, and Worried," by David Rosenberg, Merrill Lynch, May 16, 2003.
5. *Enterprise: The Dynamic of a Free People,* by Stuart Bruchey, Harvard University Press, 1990.
6. Ibid.
7. *Rainbow's End: The Crash of 1929,* by Maury Klein, Oxford University Press, 2001.
8. "Radio Part II," by Brian Trumbore, Wall Street History, Buyandhold.com.
9. "Restating the '90s," by Michael Mandel, *Business Week,* April 1, 2002.
10. Wilshire Associates. Based on e-mail correspondence.
11. "Personal Bankruptcy Filings Continue to Rise in Fiscal 2003," Administrative Office of the U.S. Courts, November 14, 2003.

12. "Deflation," by William Greider, *The Nation,* June 12, 2003.

13. *More Like Us,* by James Fallows, Houghton Mifflin, 1989.

14. "Deflation Nation," by Brian Bremner, *Business Week,* May 26, 2003.

15. *Great Depressions of the Twentieth Century,* by Edward Prescott and Timothy Kehoe, University of Minnesota.

16. "Richard Whitney" and "Charles Mitchell," by Brian Trumbore, Wall Street History, buyandhold.com.

17. "Barons of Bankruptcy," a *Financial Times* investigation, July 30, 2002.

18. Greenhodge.net weblog, Thursday, February 6, 2003.

19. "Deflation—The Poem," by Michael Silverstein, at wallstreetpoet.com.

20. "Apoplithorismosphobia," by Mark Thornton, Ludwig von Mises Institute, June 30, 2003.

CHAPTER 2: TAPS ON THE SHOULDER

1. "A global shift to deflation: A new economic era," by Eisuke Sakakibara, *International Herald Tribune,* Thursday, May 22, 2003.

2. "Letter to Shareholders," General Electric annual report, 1998.

3. *Post-Capitalist Society,* by Peter Drucker, HarperCollins, 1993.

4. *The Mind of Wall Street,* by Leon Levy with Eugene Linden, BBS Public Affairs, 2002.

5. "Is Wal-Mart Too Poweful?" by Anthony Bianco and Wendy Zellner, *Business Week,* October 6, 2003.

6. "One Nation Under Wal-Mart," by Jerry Useem, *Fortune,* March 3, 2003.

7. "How Jack Welch Runs GE," by John A. Byrne, *Business Week,* June 8, 1998.

8. "Meeting of the Federal Open Market Committee," Federal Reserve Board, December 16, 1997.

9. "Problems of Price Measurement," by Alan Greenspan,

Annual Meeting of the American Economics Association and
the American Finance Association, January 3, 1998.

10. "Dreaming With BRICs: The Path to 2050," by Dominic
Wilson and Roopa Purushothaman, Global Economics Paper
No. 99, Goldman Sachs, October 1, 2003.

CHAPTER 3: THE SUPPLY-SIDE ECONOMY

1. "Deflation: Should the Fed Be Concerned?" *The Region,*
December 2003.

2. "Is Deflation Depressing: Evidence From the Classical Gold
Standard," by Michael D. Bordo and Angela Redish, Working
Paper 9520, National Bureau of Economic Research, February
2003.

3. "The Price Is Right," by George Selgin, *National Review,*
March 23, 1998.

4. "Understanding Bob Bartley," by David Warsh,
Economicprincipals.com, December 14, 2003.

5. "Restating the '90s," by Michael Mandel, *Business Week,* April
1, 2002.

6. *The Power of Gold,* by Peter L. Bernstein, John Wiley & Sons,
2000.

7. *Monitoring the World Economy: 1820 to 1992,* by Angus
Maddison, Development Centre of the Organization for
Economic Cooperation and Development, 1995.

8. Ibid.

9. *The Communist Manifesto,* by Karl Marx and Friedrich Engels,
online text, Resources for the Study of World Civilizations,
Washington State University.

10. *The History of Money,* by Jack Weatherford, Crown Publishers,
1997.

11. "Competitiveness and the Antieconomics of Decline," by
Donald N. McCloskey, in *Second Thoughts: Myths and Morals
of U.S. Economic History,* edited by Donald McCloskey,
Oxford University Press, 1993.

12. *Theorists of Economic Growth from David Hume to the Present,* by W. W. Rostow, Oxford University Press, 1990.

13. *Industry and Empire: The Birth of the Industrial Revolution,* by Erik Hobsbawm, The New Press, 1968.

14. "Deflation," Federal Reserve Bank of Cleveland, annual report, 2002.

15. "Wyatt Earp: Desert Lawman and Adventurer," by Bob Katz, Desertusa.com.

16. *Industrializing America,* by Walter Licht, Johns Hopkins University Press, 1995.

17. *The Visible Hand: The Managerial Revolution in American Business,* by Alfred D. Chandler Jr., Belknap Press, 1993.

18. *Giants of Enterprise,* by Richard S. Tedlow, HarperBusiness, 2001.

19. *Money, Prices, and Growth,* by George Edward Dickey, Arno Press, 1997.

20. *Stocks for the Long Run,* by Jeremy J. Siegel, McGraw-Hill, 1998.

21. Jagdish Baghwati and T. N. Srinivasan, "Trade and Poverty in Poor Countries," *American Economic Review,* May 2002.

22. "China Is a Challenge and Opportunity," by Virendra Singh, Economy.com, September 23, 2003.

23. "Multinationals in China: Do They Make Money?" by Nazmeera Molla and Ed Butchart, Merrill Lynch, June 5, 2003.

CHAPTER 4: DEFLATION, AMERICAN STYLE

1. *The Great Wave: Price Revolutions and the Rhythm of History,* by David Hackett Fischer, Oxford University Press, 1996.

2. *Globalization, Growth, and Poverty: Building an Inclusive World Economy,* World Bank, 2002.

3. "It's Not a Bubble: It's a Low Frequency Revolution," by Jim Griffin, ING Investment Management, October 27, 2003.

4. "Why Are We So Afraid of Growth," by Christopher Farrell with Michael Mandel, *Business Week,* May 16, 1994.

5. "Don't Worry About Deflation: Demand for Computer Products Is Up. We Should Be Celebrating," by J. Bradford DeLong, *Wired,* August 2003.

6. "Monetary Governance in a Globalized World," by Benjamin Cohen, in Roe Goddard, Patrick Cronin, and Kishore Dash (eds.), *International Political Economy,* 2nd edition, Lynne Rienner, 2003.

7. "The IT Productivity Gap," by Erik Brynjolfsson, *Optimize,* July 2003.

8. *The End of Affluence,* by Jeffrey Madrick, Random House, 1995.

9. *Irrational Exuberance,* by Robert Shiller, Princeton University Press, 2000.

10. *dot.con,* by John Cassidy, HarperCollins, 2002.

11. "The E-Biz Surprise," by Timothy J. Mullaney, with Heather Green, Michael Arndt, Robert D. Hof, and Linda Himelstein, *Business Week,* May 12, 2003.

12. *Baumol's Cost Disease: The Arts and Other Victims,* by William Baumol, edited by Ruth Towse, Edward Elgar Publishing, 1997.

13. "What Ails Us," by James Surowiecki, *The New Yorker,* July 7, 2003.

14. "Baumol's Disease Has Been Cured: IT and Multifactor Productivity in U.S. Services Industries," by Jack E. Triplett and Barry P. Bosworth, Brookings Institution, 2002.

15. E-mail correspondence between author and Goldfinger.

16. "The Coming Skills Crisis in the American Economy," talk by Anthony Carnevale at the 2003 Workforce Development Institute, January 2003.

17. "Stunning Progress, Hidden Problems: The Dramatic Decline of Concentrated Poverty in the 1990s," by Paul A. Jargowsky, Brookings Institution, Center on Urban and Metropolitan Policy, May 2003.

18. "Dreaming with BRICs: The Path to 2050," by Dominic Wilson and Roopa Purushothaman, Global Economics Paper No. 99, Goldman Sachs, October 1, 2003.

19. *The Mind and the Market: Capitalism in Modern European Thought,* by Jerry Z. Muller, Alfred A. Knopf, 2002.

20. "Why Are We So Afraid of Growth," by Christopher Farrell with Michael Mandel, *Business Week,* May 16, 1994.

21. *The Crowd: A Study of the Popular Mind,* by Gustave Le Bon, Propaganda101.com/Online Books.

22. "Review of *Famous First Bubbles,* by Peter M. Garber," by John H. Cochrane, University of Chicago Graduate School of Business.

23. *The General Theory of Employment, Interest and Money,* by John Maynard Keynes, Harcourt Brace and Company, 1964.

24. *Famous First Bubbles: The Fundamentals of Earlier Manias,* by Peter M. Garber, MIT Press, 2001. The information and discussion of Tulipmania, the South Sea Bubble, and the Mississippi Bubble in this section mostly come from Garber.

25. *A Short History of Financial Euphoria,* by John Kenneth Galbraith, Penguin, 1994.

26. "Progress and Peril in China's Modern Economy," by Chun Chang, *The Region,* December 2003.

27. "Theory Ahead of Rhetoric: Economic Policy for a 'New Economy,'" Federal Reserve Bank of Cleveland, Annual Report, 1999.

28. *The Misunderstood Economy: What Counts and How to Count It,* by Robert Eisner, Harvard Business School Press, 1994.

CHAPTER 5: THE RISE IN INSECURITY

1. *The Gifts of Athena: Historical Origins of the Knowledge Economy,* by Joel Mokyr, Princeton University Press, 2002.

2. *The Journalism That Changed America,* edited by Judith and William Serrin, New Press, 2002.

3. *History of the American Economy,* by Gary M. Walton and Hugh Rockoff, 9th edition, Southwestern Thomson Learning, 2002.

4. *Industrializing America: The Nineteenth Century,* by Walter Licht, The Johns Hopkins University Press, 1995.

5. "The Hand That Holds the Bread: Progress and Protest," Liner Notes, New World Records and Recorded Anthology of American Music, 1978.

6. *A New Economic View of American History,* by Jeremy Attack and Peter Passell, 2nd edition, W. W. Norton & Co., 1994.

7. *Greenback,* by Jason Goodwin, Henry Holt and Company, 2003.

8. "Deflation and the Great Depression," by Stephen Smith, American Radio Works, March 1998.

9. *The Human Capital Century and American Leadership: Virtues of the Past,* by Claudia Goldin, Harvard University Press, 2001.

10. "Riding the S-Curve: Thriving in a Technological Revolution," by Jerry L. Jordan, Federal Reserve Bank of Cleveland, January 1, 2001.

11. *The Fourth Great Awakening & the Future of Egalitarianism,* by Robert William Fogel, University of Chicago Press, 2000.

12. *Money: Whence It Came, Where It Went,* by John Kenneth Galbraith, Bantam, 1976.

13. These e-mails came to me at either Soundmoney.org or Businessweek.com.

14. "Offshoring: Is It a Win-Win Game?" by Diana Farrell, McKinsey Global Institute, August 2003.

15. Business Cycles and Equilibrium, by Fisher Black, Basil Blackwell, 1987.

16. *A New Economic View of American History,* by Jeremy Attack and Peter Passell, 2nd edition, W. W. Norton & Co., 1994.

17. "Was the Deflation of 1929–30 Anticipated? The Monetary Regime as Viewed by the Business Press," by Daniel Nelson,

in Roger L. Ransom and Richard Sutch, eds., *Research in Economic History*, vol. 13, JAI Press, 1991.

18. "How Could Everyone Be So Wrong? Forecasting the Great Depression with Railroads," by Adam Klug, John S. Langdon-Lane, and Eugene White, May 2002.

19. "Waiting for Traction," by Stephen Roach, Global Economic Forum, Morgan Stanley, June 2003.

CHAPTER 6: THE GOAL OF PRICE STABILITY

1. *A History of Interest Rates,* by Sidney Homer and Richard Sylla, 3rd edition, Rutgers University Press, 1991.

2. *Nichomachean Ethics by Aristotle,* translated by W. D. Ross, the Internet Classics Archive at *classics@mit.edu.*

3. *The Annals of San Francisco,* by Frank Soulé, John H. Gihon, M.D., and James Nisbet., 1855, zpub.com.

4. *The Mind and the Market: Capitalism in Modern European Thought,* by Jerry Z. Muller, Alfred A. Knopf, 2002.

5. *A Tract on Monetary Reform,* by John Maynard Keynes, Macmillan, 1923.

6. *Essays in Persuasion,* by John Maynard Keynes, W. W. Norton, 1963.

7. "Why Do People Dislike Inflation?" by Robert J. Shiller, Yale University Press, 1996.

8. *Historical Economics,* by Charles P. Kindleberger, University of California Press, 1990.

9. *The Condition of Education 2002,* National Center for Education Statistics.

10. "The Forgotten Fourteen Million, Falling Behind in Kentucky," by John Biewen, American RadioWorks, May 1999.

11. "I Look at a DVD Player for $42.99 and Worry," by Mike Langberg, *San Jose Mercury News,* May 25, 2003.

12. "Deflation: Making Sure 'It' Doesn't Happen Here," by Ben S.

Bernanke, National Economists Club, Washington, D.C., November 21, 2002.

13. *The Cultural Contradictions of Capitalism,* by Daniel Bell, Basic Books, 1976.

14. "The Inflation Target 10 Years On," by Mervyn King, London School of Economics, November 19, 2002.

15. *Hamilton's Blessing: The Extraordinary Life and Times of Our National Debt,* by John Steele Gordon, Walker and Company, 1997.

16. *History of the American Economy,* by Gary M. Walton and Hugh Rockoff, 9th edition, Southwestern Thomson Learning, 2002.

17. "U.S. Securities Markets and the Banking System, 1790–1840," by Richard Sylla, review, Federal Reserve Bank of St. Louis, May/June, 1998.

18. "Gold, Fiat Money and Price Stability," By Michael D. Bordo, Robert Dittmar, and William T. Galvin, Working Paper 2003-014, June 2003.

19. Two wonderful and detailed recountings of Morgan's role in the 1907 panic are *The House of Morgan: An American Banking Dynasty and the Rise of Modern Finance,* by Ron Chernow, Simon & Schuster, 1990; and *Morgan: American Financier,* by Jean Strouse, Random House, 1999.

CHAPTER 7: "BAD" DEFLATIONS

1. "Interview with Alan Meltzer," *The Region,* September 2003.

2. *Essays in Persuasion,* by John Maynard Keynes, W. W. Norton, 1963.

3. *Enterprise: The Dynamic of a Free People,* by Stuart Bruchey, Harvard University Press, 1990, and *History of the American Economy,* by Gary M. Walton and Hugh Rockoff, 9th edition, Southwestern Thomson Learning, 2002.

4. "Hard Times: An Oral History of the Great Depression," by

Studs Terkel, 1973 broadcast, Studs Terkel Program, WFMT radio.

5. *Colossus,* edited by Jack Beatty, Broadway Books, 2001.

6. *History of the American Economy,* by Gary M. Walton and Hugh Rockoff, 9th edition, Southwestern Thomson Learning, 2002.

7. "Deflation," Federal Reserve Bank of Cleveland, Annual Report, 2002.

8. "The Gold Standard and the Great Depression," by Barry Eichengreen and Peter Temin, Working Paper 6060, National Bureau of Economic Research, June 1997.

9. Ibid.

10. *The Great Contraction 1929–1933,* by Milton Friedman and Anna Jacobson Schwartz, Princeton University Press, 1965.

11. Ibid.

12. "The Gold Standard and the Great Depression," by Barry Eichengreen and Peter Temin, Working Paper 6060, National Bureau of Economic Research, June 1997.

13. " 'Liquidation' Cycles and the Great Depression," by J. Brad DeLong, June 1991.

14. Ibid.

15. "The Macroeconomics of the Great Depression: A Comparative Approach," by Ben Bernanke (Money, Credit, and Banking Lecture), *Journal of Money, Credit, and Banking,* February 1995, vol. 27, no. 1. "Macroeconomics Priorities," by Robert E. Lucas, Jr. American Economics Association Presidential Address, January, 2003

CHAPTER 8: THE GREAT INFLATION

1. "History of the G.I. Bill," Utah Valley State College, Graduation and Transfer Services.

2. *People of Plenty,* by David Potter, University of Chicago Press, 1954.

3. *Modern Capitalism: The Changing Balance of Public and Private Power,* by Andrew Shonfield, Oxford University Press, 1965.

4. "An Inflation Generation," by Lawrence K. Roos, Federal Reserve Bank of St. Louis, May 18, 1980.

5. "The World Turned Upside Down: An End to Inflation?" by Chris Farrell, American RadioWorks, March 18, 1998.

6. "Inflation and Its Discontents," by Michael Boskin, American Economic Association/American Finance Association Joint Luncheon Address, *Hoover Essays in Public Policy,* 1997.

7. "Inflation?" by Peter Bernstein, Economics and Portfolio Strategy, December 1, 2001.

8. "America's Historical Experience with Low Inflation," by J. Brad DeLong, November 30, 1999.

9. "Bretton Woods System," by Benjamin Cohen, in *Routledge Encyclopedia of International Political Economy,* edited by R. J. Barry Jones, Routledge, 2002.

10. "Business Cycles in a Financially Deregulated America," by Albert M. Wojnilower, in *Monetary Theory as a Basis for Monetary Policy,* edited by Axel Leijonhufvud, Palgrave, 2001.

11. *The Organization Man,* by William Whyte, University of Pennsylvania Press, 2002.

12. *The New Industrial State,* by John Kenneth Galbraith, Houghton Mifflin, 1967.

13. *Capital Ideas,* by Peter Bernstein, Free Press, 1992.

14. "An Inflation Generation," by Lawrence K. Roos, Federal Reserve Bank of St. Louis, May 18, 1980.

15. *Inside the Fed: Making Monetary Policy,* by William C. Melton, Dow Jones–Irwin, 1985.

16. *The Cultural Contradictions of Capitalism,* by Daniel Bell, Basic Books, 1976.

17. "Why Do People Dislike Inflation?" by Robert J. Shiller, Yale University Press, 1996.

18. *Essays in Persuasion,* by John Maynard Keynes, W. W. Norton, 1963.

19. "Bretton Woods System," by Benjamin Cohen, in R. J. Barry Jones, ed., *Routledge Encyclopedia of International Political Economy,* Routledge, 2002.

20. *The Great American Bond Market: Selected Speeches of Sidney Homer,* Dow Jones–Irwin, 1978.

21. "What Pendulums Do," by David Warsh, Economicprincipals.com, May 25, 2003.

22. *Giants of Enterprise: Seven Business Innovators and the Empires They Built,* by Richard Tedlow, HarperBusiness, 2001.

CHAPTER 9: BUSINESS AND WORKERS IN AN ERA OF FIERCE PRICE COMPETITION

1. *The Progress Paradox: How Life Gets Better While People Feel Worse,* by Greg Easterbrook, Random House, 2003.

2. *History of the Decline and Fall of the Roman Empire,* by Edward Gibbon, Cryptomaoist edition, Gutenberg Project, 1966.

3. *The Progress Paradox,* by Greg Easterbrook, Random House, 2003.

4. "Happiness: Does Social Science Have a Clue?" by Richard Layard, Lionel Robbins Memorial Lectures 2002/3, March 2003.

5. "Layoff Survival Kit," by *Right on the Money* host Chris Farrell, 2002.

6. "Dell," by Andrew Park, The Web Smart 50: The Cutting Edge, *Business Week,* November 24, 2003.

7. "You Won the Brokerage War," by Steven T. Goldberg, *Kiplinger Personal Finance Magazine,* August 1999.

8. "Giant Sucking Sound," by Robyn Meredith, *Forbes,* September 29, 2003.

9. "More Corporate Challenges Ahead," by John T. Slania, *Crains' Chicago Business,* October 20, 2003.

10. "Issues Related to Competition and Subscriber Rates in the Cable Television Industry," Government Accounting Office, GAO-04-8, October 2003.

11. "Choosing the Wrong Pricing Strategy Can Be a Costly Mistake," by Jagmohan Raju and Z. John Zhang, Knowledge @ Wharton Newsletter, June 4, 2003.

12. "Intangible Assets: Computers and Organizational Capital," by Erik Brynjolfsson, Lorin M. Hitt, and Shinkyu Yang, Working Paper 138, 2002.

13. *Downsizing in America: Reality, Causes, and Consequences,* by William J. Baumol, Alan S. Blinder, and Edward N. Wolff, Russell Sage Foundation, 2003.

CHAPTER 10: WHAT KIND OF RETURN CAN INVESTORS EXPECT?

1. "Silver Blaze," by Sir Arthur Conan Doyle, in *The Complete Sherlock Holmes,* Gramercy, 2002.

2. "Financial Markets in 2020," by Charles S. Sanford Jr., Federal Reserve Bank of Kansas City Economic Symposium, August 1993.

3. "Money Where You Work," by *Right on the Money* host Chris Farrell, 1999.

4. "Global Financial Data Guide to Total Returns on Stocks, Bonds and Bills," by Dr. Bryan Taylor, president, Global Financial Data, Inc.

5. *It Was a Very Good Year: Extraordinary Moments in Stock Market History,* by Martin S. Fridson, John Wiley & Sons, 1998.

6. Niall Ferguson's Database at pages.stern.nyu.edu/~rsylla/.

7. *Tuxedo Park,* by Jennet Conant, Simon & Schuster, 2002.

8. "Deflation . . . What If?" by Eric Bjorgen and Andy Engel, edited by Steve Leuthold, The Leuthold Group, December 2002.

9. "Where Is the Market Going? Uncertain Facts and Novel

Theories," by John Cochrane, *Economic Perspectives* XXI: 6 (November/December 1997), Federal Reserve Bank of Chicago.

10. *Irrational Exuberance,* by Robert Shiller, Princeton University Press, 2000.

11. Ibid.

12. "What Risk Premium Is 'Normal'?" by Robert D. Arnott and Peter L. Bernstein, Association for Investment Management and Research, March/April 2002.

13. *The Random Walk Guide to Investing: Ten Rules for Financial Success,* by Burton Malkiel, W. W. Norton, 2003.

14. *Business Cycles and Equilibrium,* by Fisher Black, Basil Blackwell, 1987.

15. "Trading Is Hazardous to Your Wealth: The Common Stock Performance of Individual Investors," by Terrance Odean and Brad Barber, *Journal of Finance,* LV(2), April 2000.

16. *Restoring Trust: Financial Services in the New Era,* by John Bogle, SunGard World, September 2003.

17. Shareholder Letter, Berkshire Hathaway, by Warren Buffett, 1993.

18. Conversation with Karl E. Case, professor at Wellesley.

19. "Why a Crash Wouldn't Cripple the Economy," by Gary Becker, *Business Week,* April 14, 1997.

CHAPTER 11: THE NEW REGIME AND PUBLIC POLICY

1. "Deflation: Should the Fed Be Concerned?" *The Region,* December 2003.

2. "New Goods, Old Theory, and the Welfare Costs of Trade Restrictions," by Paul Romer, *Journal of Development Economics* 43, 1994.

3. Remarks of Harvard University president Lawrence H. Summers, Nieman Narrative Journalism Conference, November 10, 2002.

4. "Who Bought the Farm," by Chris Farrell, American Radio-Works, March 2002.

5. "Should the Government Subsidize Supply or Demand in the Market for Scientists and Engineers?" by Paul Romer, NBER Working Paper 7723, May 2000.

6. "Is Technological Change in Medicine Worth It?" by David Cutler and Mark McClellan, *Health Affairs*, 20(5), September/October 2001.

7. "Are the Benefits of Newer Drugs Worth Their Cost? Evidence from the 1996 MEPS," by Frank Lichtenberg, *Health Affairs* 20(5), September/October 2001.

8. "The Workforce Investment Act: Reauthorization to Address the 'Skills Gap,' by Harry J. Holzer and Margy Waller, the Brookings Institution, research brief, December 2003.

9. "Structural Change in the New Economy," by Alan Greenspan, National Governors' Association, 92nd annual meeting, State College, Pennsylvania, July 11, 2000.

10. "The Human Capital Century and American Leadership: Virtues of the Past," by Claudia Goldin, *Journal of Economic History*, June 2001.

11. "State Fiscal Constraints and Higher Education Spending," by Thomas Kane and David Gunter, Urban-Brookings Tax Policy Center Discussion Paper No. 12, May 2003.

12. "Should the Government Subsidize Supply or Demand in the Market for Scientists and Engineers?" by Paul Romer, NBER Working Paper 7723, May 2000.

13. "Commentary: Is There a Role for Discretionary Fiscal Policy?" by Martin Feldstein, symposium sponsored by the Federal Reserve Bank of Kansas City, August 29–31, 2002.

14. *Capitalism and Freedom*, by Milton Friedman, University of Chicago Press, 2002.

Index